PEAK

ROLAND SMITH

Houghton Mifflin Harcourt
Boston New York

Text set in Plantin
Cover design by Francis Floro
Book design by April Ward

This is a work of fiction. All the names, characters, organizations, and events portrayed in this book are products of the author's imagination. Any resemblance to any organization, event, or actual person, living or dead, is unintentional.

Printed in the U.S.A.

ISBN 978-0-545-88217-0

2 3 4 5 6 7 8 9 10 23 24 23 22 21 20 19 18 17 16

513818

This book is for Marie, for giving me all the things that matter

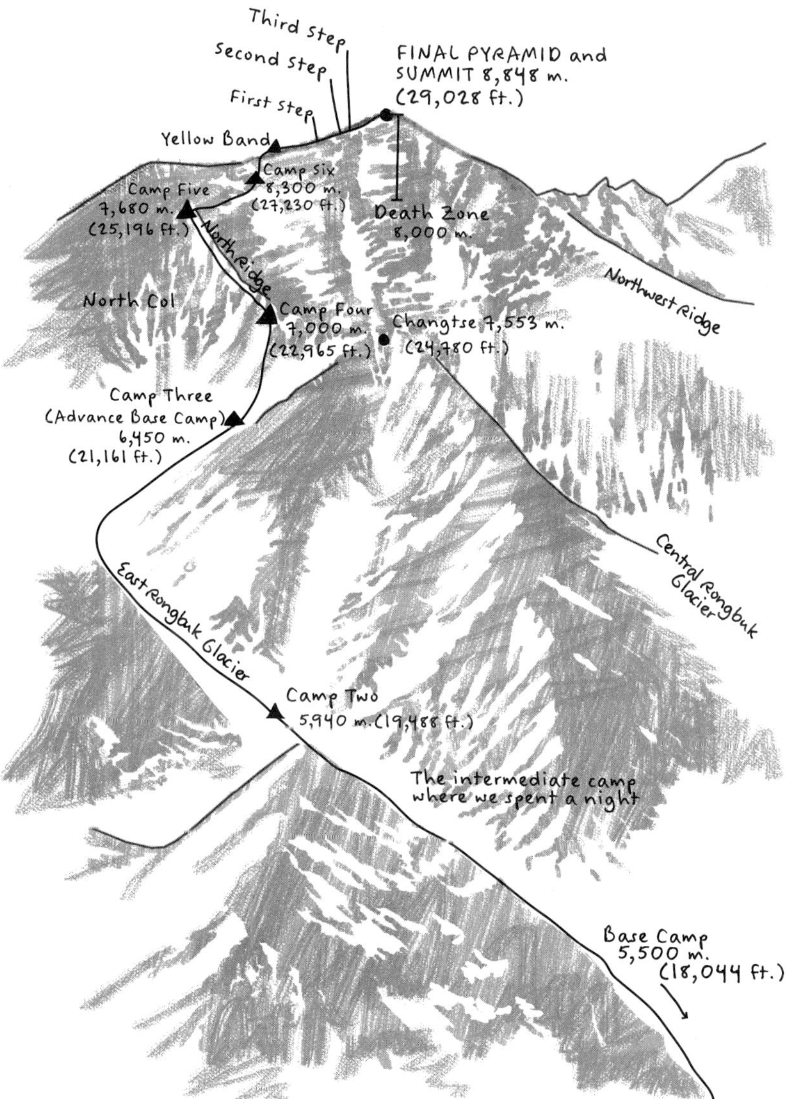

My route up the northern side of Everest

MULES

KINE #1

THE ASSIGNMENT

MY NAME IS PEAK. Yeah, I know: weird name. But you don't get to pick your name or your parents. (Or a lot of other things in life for that matter.) It could have been worse. My parents could have named me Glacier, or Abyss, or Crampon. I'm not kidding. According to my mom all those names were on the list.

Vincent, my literary mentor (at your school this would be your English teacher), asked me to write this for my year-end assignment (no grades at our school).

When Vincent reads the sentence you just read he'll say: *Peak, that is a run-on sentence and chaotically parenthetical.* (That's how he talks.) Meaning it's a little confusing and choppy. And I'll tell him that my life is (parenthetical) and the chaos is due to the fact that I'm starting this assignment in the back of a Toyota pickup in Tibet (aka China) with an automatic pencil that doesn't have an eraser and it's not likely that I'm going to find an eraser around here.

Vincent has also said that a good writer should draw the reader in by starting in the middle of the story with a *hook,* then go back and fill in what happened before the *hook.*

Once you have the reader hooked you can write whatever you want as you slowly reel them in.

I guess Vincent thinks readers are fish. If that's the case, most of Vincent's fish have gotten away. He's written something like twenty literary novels, all of which are out of print. If he knew what he was talking about why do I have to search the dark, moldering aisles of used-book stores to find his books?

(Now I've done it. But remember this, Vincent: *Writers should tell the brutal truth in their own voice and not let individuals, society, or consequences dictate their words!* And you thought no one was listening to you in class. You also know that I really like your books, or I wouldn't waste my time trying to find them. Nor would I be trying to get this story down in the back of a truck in Tibet.)

Speaking of which . . .

This morning we slowed down to get around a boulder the size of a school bus that had fallen in the middle of the road. In the U.S.A. we would use dynamite or heavy equipment to move it. In Tibet they use picks, sledgehammers, and prisoners in tattered, quilted coats to chip the boulder down to nothing. The prisoners smiled at us as we tried not to run over their shackled feet on the narrow road. Their cheerful faces were covered in nicks and cuts from rock shrapnel. Those not chipping used crude wooden wheelbarrows to move the man-made gravel over to potholes, where very old Tibetan prisoners used battered shovels and rakes to fill in the holes. Chinese soldiers in green uniforms and with rifles slung over their shoulders stood around fifty-gallon burn barrels smoking cigarettes. The prisoners looked happier than the soldiers did.

I wondered if the boulder would be gone by the time I came back through. I wondered if I'd ever come back through.

THE HOOK

I WAS ONLY TWO-THIRDS up the wall when the sleet started to freeze onto the black terra-cotta.

My fingers were numb. My nose was running. I didn't have a free hand to wipe my nose, or enough rope to rappel about five hundred feet to the ground. I had planned everything out so carefully, except for the weather, and now it was uh-oh time.

A gust of wind tried to peel me off the wall. I dug my fingers into the seam and hugged the terra-cotta until it passed.

I should have waited until June to make the ascent, but no, moron has to go up in March. Why? Because everything was ready and I have a problem with waiting. I had studied the wall, built all my custom protection, and picked the date. I was ready. And if the date passed I might not try it at all. It doesn't take much to talk yourself out of a stunt like this. That's why there are over six billion people sitting safely inside homes and one . . .

"Moron!" I shouted.

Option #1: Finish the climb. Two hundred sixty-four feet up, or about a hundred precarious fingerholds (providing my fingers didn't break off like icicles).

Option #2: Climb down. A little over five hundred feet, two hundred fifty fingerholds.

Option #3: Wait for rescue. Scratch that option. No one knew I was on the wall. By morning (providing someone actually looked up and saw me) I would be an icy gargoyle. And if I lived my mom would drop me off the wall herself.

Up it is, then.

I timed my moves between vicious blasts of wind, which were becoming more frequent the higher I climbed. The sleet turned to hail, pelting me like a swarm of frozen hornets. But the worst happened about thirty feet from the top, fifteen measly fingerholds away.

I had stopped to give the lactic acid searing my shoulders and arms a chance to simmer down. I was mouth breathing (partly from exertion, partly from terror), and I told myself I would make the final push as soon as I caught my breath.

While I waited, a thick mist drifted in around me. The top of the wall disappeared, which was just as well. When you're tired and scared, thirty feet looks about the length of two football fields, and that can be pretty demoralizing. Scaling a wall happens one foothold and one handhold at a time. Thinking beyond that can weaken your resolve, and it's your will that gets you to the top as much as your muscles and climbing skills.

Finally, I started breathing through my runny nose again. Kind of snorting, really, but I was able to close my mouth every other breath.

This is it, I told myself. *Fifteen more handholds and I've topped it.*

I reached up for the next seam and encountered a little snag. Well, a big snag really . . .

My right ear and cheek were frozen to the wall.

To reach the top you must have resolve, muscles, skill, and . . .

A FACE!

Mine was anchored to that wall like a bolt, and a portion of it stayed there when I gathered enough *resolve* to tear it loose. Now I was mad, which was exactly what I needed to finish the climb.

Cursing with every vertical lunge, I stopped about four feet below the edge, tempted to tag this monster with the blood running down my neck. But instead I took the mountain stencil out of my pack (cheating, I know, but you have to have two free hands to do it freehand), slapped it on the wall, and filled it in with blue spray paint.

This is when the helicopter came up behind me and nearly blew me off the wall.

"You are under arrest!" an amplified voice shouted above the deafening rotors.

I looked down. Most of the mist had been swirled away by the chopper rotors, and for the first time in an hour I could see the busy street eight hundred feet below the skyscraper.

A black rope dropped down next to me, and two alarmed and angry faces leaned over the edge of the roof.

"Take the rope!"

I wasn't about to take the rope four feet away from my goal. I started up.

"Take the rope!"

When my head reached the top of the railing they hauled me up and cuffed my wrists behind my back. They were wearing SWAT gear and NYPD baseball caps, and there were a lot of them.

One of the cops leaned close to my bloody ear. “What were you thinking?” he said, then jerked me to my feet and handed me off to a regular street cop.

“Get this moron to emergency.”

A COUPLE OF STITCHES & THE SLAMMER

WHEN I STEPPED OUT of the elevator into the lobby I was shocked by the swarm of reporters with flashing cameras. How did they get there so quickly?

"He's just a kid."

"What's your name?"

"He's bleeding."

"Why'd you do it?"

"Did you make it to the top?"

I didn't answer any of their questions. In fact, I barely looked at them. The whole point of a spectacular tag is not the artwork; it's the mystery of how it was done.

A subway rider goes by the same seventeen abandoned freight cars parked on a sidetrack, week after week, year after year, then one morning all seventeen of them have been tagged top to bottom with wild beautiful graffiti. Or a driver in bumper-to-bumper traffic drives under the same overpass a thousand times, barely noticing it, until the morning the entire span is painted Day-Glo orange and green.

How'd they do that?

Scaffolds?

In one night?

How many of them were there?

Where were the cops?

What's the point?

The mystery. That's the point. And there isn't enough of it, in my opinion.

My little blue mountains were small, but I made up for their size by putting them in audacious places where they might never be seen except by a bored office worker or window washer. This was my sixth skyscraper. I had planned to do nine all together. Why? I have no idea. Now everyone would know how I did it. The mystery was gone and that was the worst part of getting caught.

Or so I thought.

I expected my mom to show up in the emergency room and tear off my left ear, but she didn't. (And it turned out that my right ear was still attached to my head, as was most of my cheek.)

The East Indian emergency doc took a look at my face under the light for a minute or two, then asked me what happened, eyeing the two cops standing in the doorway as if they were the ones who had messed me up.

"My face froze to a wall."

"You should have used lukewarm water to unfreeze it."

"If I'd had some handy I would have."

"I'm going to clean it up and put in a couple of little stitches."

I was out of there in less than an hour. The two cops drove me to the police station and put me in a filthy room with a two-way mirror. I didn't look so hot. I didn't feel so good, either. My head throbbed. My arms and legs ached. And I had four fingernails split all the way down the middle. It felt like someone had lit them on fire. The emergency doc hadn't even bothered to look at them.

After what seemed like two days the door opened and a

tired-looking detective in a rumpled suit came in carrying my backpack and a thick file. He dumped the contents of the pack on the table and went through everything piece by piece. When he finished he scooped the stuff back in, then looked at me and shook his head.

"You messed up, Pete."

"Peak," I said.

"Like in 'mountain peak'?"

"Right."

"Weird name."

"Weird parents."

"Yeah, I just talked with your mother. She said that I had her permission to beat you to death."

Good old Mom.

"I got another phone call," he added. "The mayor. I've been a cop for thirty-five years, and I've never gotten a personal call from the mayor. He's upset. Turns out he was at a reception in the Woolworth Building. They thought you were a terrorist, but it's pretty clear now that you're just a moron."

He stared at me, waiting for a reaction. I didn't give him one. I *was* a moron. I should have checked the building's evening schedule more carefully before I scaled it. The reporters hadn't rushed over to snap photos of me. They were already there for the mayor's reception, and so were the cops.

"They'll take you over to JDC in a bit."

"What's JDC?" I hadn't been arrested before.

"Juvenile Detention Center. You'll stay there until you're arraigned."

I wasn't sure what that meant, either, and the detective must have sensed this because he explained that there was a separate court system for juvenile defendants. The district attorney would decide what the charges would be and I would have to go before a judge and plead guilty or not guilty.

"Then they'll let me out," I said.

"Maybe, maybe not. Depends on how much the bail is and whether your parents can cough up the dough. Or, they might deny bail all together, which means you'll be in JDC until your trial or sentencing date. That could be months. The courts are backed up."

My mouth went dry.

"I haven't been in trouble before," I said.

"You mean you haven't been caught before." The detective opened the file folder and spread out three photographs on the table. "We've been tracking these tags for quite a while now. Looks like we caught the tagger red-handed."

The photos were grainy, obviously taken with a long telephoto lens, but the blue stenciled mountains were clear enough.

Two uniformed cops were waiting for me outside the interrogation room along with my mom, who was so mad she could barely speak. She looked at the bandages on my face and managed to ask if I was okay.

"Yeah, I'm fine."

"We've got to take him to JDC, ma'am," one of the cops said.

Mom nodded, then looked at me. "We'll see what we can do, Peak. But you've really done it this time."

The cops led me away.

BY THE THIRD DAY at JDC I was climbing the wall (literally) until my counselor (that's what they call the guards here) told me to stop.

Spider Boy, Fly Boy, The Gecko Kid was front-page news every morning. Each article dug deeper and deeper into my family's past: my mom, dad, stepfather, even my twin sisters were targets. There were infrared photos of me clinging to the scraper, photos from school, photos of my mom and dad when they were rock rats. And my other two blue mountain tags had been discovered.

I stopped reading the newspaper accounts after the second day and left the common room when the news came on the television.

They limited our phone calls at JDC. I was only able to catch Mom once to ask her what was going on, but she was meeting with the attorneys and didn't have time to talk.

On the morning of the fourth day my counselor came into my room (that's what they call the cells) and said I had a visitor. Finally!

I was pretty disappointed to see it was Vincent in the visiting room instead of my mom. (No offense, Vincent.) He looked a little shocked when he saw my scabbed-over face and ear.

"I brought some books for you to read," he said, pushing a couple of paperbacks across the table. "I imagine it gets a bit boring in here."

"Yeah. Thanks."

"I also brought along a couple Moleskine notebooks." He took two black, shrink-wrapped notebooks out of his bag and set them on the table like they were sacred texts. "They are made in Italy. Van Gogh, Picasso, Ernest Hemingway, Bruce Chatwin drew or wrote in Moleskines."

"Really?"

I guess I'd better tell you a little more about my school.

It's a special school. In fact, so special that it doesn't have an official name. It's simply known as the Greene Street School, or GSS, because that's the street it's on. There are one hundred students, kindergarten through high school, from all over Manhattan. Most of the kids are prodigies—meaning they play music, sing, dance, act, solve math problems computers can't solve—and me . . . who can't do any of these things. I got in because of my stepfather, Rolf Young. He's on their advisory board and does all of their legal work pro bono, meaning for free. The school is two blocks from our loft, and my twin sisters go there, too, but unlike me, they deserve to be there. They are both piano wizards.

It took them a year to figure out my talent, which I think they made up so Rolf would continue to do stuff for free.

"Peak is our writer!" the headmistress declared one day, holding up an essay I'd scrawled out that morning as I gulped down a bowl of cereal before leaving for school.

I would have preferred to be their climber, but GSS doesn't recognize sports as a worthy human endeavor.

Don't get me wrong, I like GSS. The students and teachers are a quirky bunch and wildly entertaining. I've even managed to learn some things there. The problem is that I don't have any friends at the school. This isn't anyone's fault, really. My main interest is climbing. The other students are interested in things like number theory, what kind of gut to use on their violin or cello bows, and painting techniques.

Anyway, this is how I got hooked up with Vincent. As the school's English teacher he got stuck with the job of mentoring the alleged writer.

He unwrapped one of the Moleskines and showed me

how there was a little pocket in back to store notes and how the elastic band stretched to mark your place or hold the notebook closed.

"I brought you a pen," he said. "But they would not let me give it to you. They were afraid you would write on your wall with it."

I think they were probably more afraid that I would use it to stab somebody (or more likely someone would take it away and stab me with it).

"I will see what I can do about getting you something to write with," Vincent said. He always spoke slowly, enunciating each word precisely, and I had never heard him use a contraction. "Some of the best literature ever written was composed inside prison cells."

I didn't plan on being at JDC long enough to compose anything.

"Whether you come back to school or not, you can still complete this year. I have talked to the headmistress. Four other authors and I will evaluate you by the words you put in the notebook."

Evaluate meant graduate at GSS.

"I brought you two Moleskines in case you write a longer piece. It must be a story—not a diary, or a journal—with a beginning, middle, and a denouement at the end to tie the story together. The story can be based on your life, someone else's life, or events completely from your imagination. You only have to complete one of the Moleskines to fulfill your requirement, using some of the writing techniques I have taught you during the past year."

"I'm coming back to school," I said.

He didn't look like he believed me.

"Regardless," he said. "The assignment will remain the same."

LATER THAT MORNING I had a second visitor. A woman. Long brown hair, pale blue eyes, olive-colored skin, carrying a garment bag. She was short, but powerfully built, with good muscle tone in her arms. Aside from a slight stiffness in her back (which you'd have to know her to notice), the only flaw she had were her hands. They were scarred from years of climbing.

"Sorry I couldn't get out here sooner," Mom said. "With the twins, and the attorneys, and—"

"That's okay," I interrupted. JDC was at least an hour-and-a-half drive from our loft in Manhattan. In addition to everything else, Mom worked full-time at a bookstore she and a friend owned. Still, I would have liked to have seen her before this.

She walked over to where I was sitting and looked at the scabs on my face.

"Ugly," she said.

"Thanks."

She started pacing.

"How are the twins?"

"They haven't stopped crying since you got busted."

I winced. It was one thing to upset my mom, but I didn't like upsetting Patrice and Paula. "Two peas in a pod," as Mom and Rolf called them, or "Pea-Pea" as I called them, which always made them giggle. They were six years old and looked up to the third "Pea" (me) like I was a god.

"You've really done it this time, Peak. Six skyscrapers!

They're going to eat you up and spit you out. Rolf has cashed in every favor he has in the city, but I don't think any of it is going to work. He got your arraignment delayed, and tried for a second delay . . ."

(I had seen my mom agitated before, but I had never seen her like this. She was pacing the small holding cell like a caged leopard.)

". . . hoping that the publicity would die down, but after last night that's all down the tube. The district attorney, who Rolf went to school with, and the judge nixed that idea—"

"Wait," I said. "What happened last night?"

She stopped pacing and glared at me with her mouth open and her eyes wide.

"You didn't hear?"

I shook my head.

"A boy fell from the Flatiron Building. He's dead."

I stared at her. "What does that have—"

"To do with you?" she yelled. "It's *because* of you, Peak. The boy had all your news articles pinned up in his bedroom. He had a can of blue spray paint in his pack. He had never been climbing in his entire life, which explains why he only made it up seventy-five feet. But the fall was enough to kill him, and enough to keep you in jail for the next three years."

"What?" I was on my feet now.

"Unbelievable!" She let out a harsh laugh. "You're circling the drain, Peak, and you don't even know it."

Circling the drain—a term from our past lives out West. I hadn't heard it in years.

"What do you mean 'three years'?"

"And three months," she said. "That's when you'll be eighteen."

I started pacing now. All I did was climb the Woolworth Building. I didn't brag about it or post it on the Internet. It was my little secret. My way of... Well, I didn't know exactly why I had done it. I felt bad about the other boy, but it wasn't my fault.

"Did you tell Dad?" I asked, meaning my real dad, not Rolf.

This elicited another harsh laugh.

"He's in Nepal. I left him a message with a Sherpa who barely spoke a word of English. I'm not even sure why I called him. Desperation, I guess."

She took a deep breath. "Look, I have to go. Rolf and I are meeting with the attorneys."

"Attorneys?" I thought Rolf would be my attorney.

"Two of them. Rolf can't represent you. He's your stepfather, conflict of interest."

"Do you think—"

Her whole demeanor changed when she noticed how scared I was. She softened and her pale blue eyes filled with tears.

"I hope so, Peak," she said quietly. "But I'm not optimistic. The city wants to make an example out of you." She turned away and wiped her eyes, then handed me the garment bag. "This is a suit. You'll have to wear it tomorrow. And I talked to them downstairs. A barber is going to come in and cut your hair sometime this afternoon."

I sat down heavily in the chair.

"Buck up," she said with strained cheerfulness. "I don't think he'll butcher your hair too badly. You've got to look like you're—"

"I'm not worried about my hair! I'm worried about those three years. I'm already going crazy in here. I can't—"

It all hit me at once: the climb, the arrest, the kid falling from the Flatiron. . . . I broke down.

My mom held me.

CIRCLING THE DRAIN

I COULD TIE A BACHMAN, bowline, butterfly, figure eight, double fisherman, and a half dozen other knots with one hand in the dark, but I couldn't get the tie knotted properly around my neck. The few times I'd worn one, Rolf had done the honors. The guard assigned to escort me to the courtroom finally came to my rescue. Between us, we figured it out, then he led me into the courtroom.

Sitting at a table to the left of the bench were the prosecuting attorneys (a man and a woman) shuffling papers, barely looking up at the person whose life they were about to ruin.

At the table to the right were my attorneys (another man and a woman). They too were shuffling papers, but they stopped when the guard passed me off to them, smiling, shaking my hand, introducing themselves. . . .

I didn't quite catch their names. I was too busy staring at the five people sitting behind them. Rolf, looking dapper and professional with a perfectly knotted tie. Next to him were Patrice and Paula. They were a little teary-eyed, but excited to see me, wearing their favorite dresses. (Matching of course.) They waved and tried to stifle giggles when I mouthed "Pea-Pea" at them. (Don't get me wrong: I wasn't in a joking mood at that moment, but I felt the twins could use a boost. They had been through enough the past few days.)

Next to the twins was my mom, looking worried, but distinctly more relaxed than she had been at JDC the day before. Maybe this was because of the guy sitting next to her. (Although I doubted it.)

His name was Joshua Wood—arguably the greatest mountaineer in the world. He was also my father.

I hadn't seen him in seven years and he looked about as comfortable in his suit as I felt in mine. He had shaved his trademark beard. (Recently, by the looks of it.) The skin beneath was pale compared to the upper part of his handsome face, which was windburned and sunburned. His lips were chapped and his nose was peeling, giving him the overall look of someone who had just been dug out from under an avalanche.

His eyes were the same pale blue as my mother's. He gave me a nod and a smile, which I was too stunned to return.

"All rise," the bailiff said, startling me out of my stupor.

One of the attorneys turned me around and gave me a dazzling smile. I expected her to say, "Love the tie." But what she said instead was, "Don't say one word unless I tell you to. Act remorseful."

She was obviously my lead attorney. I thought her name was Traci.

The judge—a tough-looking guy with a white crew cut—took his seat behind the bench and made us stand for a few seconds more before nodding at the bailiff.

"Be seated," the bailiff said with a slight quiver in his voice.

My mom was right: The judge was going to eat me up and spit me out. He put on a pair of glasses and went over some notes, then started reading the charges aloud. "Criminal trespass, vandalism, reckless endangerment . . ."

It went on and on.

Finally reaching the end of the list, he pushed his glasses to the end of his nose and looked over the top of them directly at me. "How do you plead?"

Traci pulled me to my feet and whispered the answer in my ear. I wasn't sure I had heard her right. She whispered it again with the same smile plastered on her face from before.

I took a deep breath.

"Not guilty," I said.

"To all charges?" the judge asked incredulously.

"That's right, Your Honor," Traci answered, her smile unwavering.

"You've gotta be kidding me. The state has videotape of him climbing the Woolworth Building. There were twenty-three cops on the roof that saw him being pulled over the railing. He signed a statement attesting to the facts."

"Duress," Traci said. "He was exhausted, injured, and half frozen at the time."

"Oh please. This kid has received absolutely every consideration the system can offer, including delaying this arraignment. Now, what's this all about?"

"We want to go to trial," Traci answered.

The arteries in the judge's neck looked like they were about to burst. He glared over at the prosecutors' table. "Do you two know anything about this?"

The prosecutors shook their heads, vigorously.

"Perhaps we should retire to your chambers," one of them suggested.

"Yes," Traci agreed cheerfully.

"The four of you crammed into my office," the judge

said. "Forget it. There's no one here but . . ." He noticed Patrice and Paula sitting between my mom and Rolf.

"Oh," he said, then looked over at the guard who had brought me down in the elevator.

"Do you think you can take these young ladies out and find them some ice cream?"

"What about the prisoner?" the guard asked.

"I think he'll hang around for this." He looked at the twins. "Do you like ice cream?"

"Chocolate," Paula said.

"Vanilla," Patrice said.

"I think that can be arranged."

"Do you want us to bring you back some, Peak?" Paula asked.

"I bet they have strawberry," Patrice said (my favorite), but it sounded like "awe-berry" because she had recently lost her front teeth.

"Nah," I said. "I had a big bowl for breakfast."

"You did not!" they said in unison, giggling, as the guard took them out.

The judge waited for the door to swing completely closed before continuing the proceedings. He nodded at the court reporter. "We're off the record."

She turned off her recorder and stopped typing.

"It's just us now," the judge continued, looking at Traci. "You know as well as I do that we don't want to go to trial with this. It's turned into a media circus. A boy was killed two days ago. I'm sure you and Peak and his parents don't want that to happen again."

"Of course not," Traci said. "But by the same token I

can't let my client be unfairly incarcerated because the media is out of control. This whole thing has not been handled well by the police department or the mayor's office."

The judge looked at her for a moment, then looked over at the prosecutors. "She makes a good point. What do you think?"

The older of the two prosecutors (the woman) stood. "Prior to the arraignment we offered a plea bargain of two years with six months off for good behavior. Eighteen months is a pretty good deal considering the charges."

Not if you're serving it, I thought. But it was better than three years. Traci picked up a sheet of paper from the table.

"In the last five years, fifteen adults have been arrested for climbing skyscrapers in New York City. The longest sentence has been six months, and several of these climbers served no time at all." She looked at the prosecutor. "We can beat this in court. We're going to trial."

The prosecutor gave her a sour look.

I felt the drain being plugged, but it wasn't watertight yet.

"What's your bottom line?" the judge asked.

"A fine with probation," Traci answered. "And no time served."

"Forget it," the judge said gruffly.

"What if we could arrange for Peak to leave New York today?" Traci asked. "Out of sight, out of mind, out of the newspaper. No interviews. The story dies because the story is gone. Poof!"

The judge almost smiled. "A disappearing act, huh? Explain."

"Peak's biological father has offered to take custody of him."

I whipped around so fast I hurt my neck.

My father had gotten to his feet.

"I take it you're the father?"

"Yes, sir. Joshua Wood."

"The climber?"

"Yes, sir."

The judge glanced at Rolf and Mom, then looked back at Joshua. "Mr. Wood, how much time have you spent with your son lately?"

"Not much the past few years," he admitted.

Not any for the last seven years to be exact, I thought.

"When Teri and Rolf got married," he continued, "we decided it would be best for Peak if I kept a low profile."

This was the first time I'd heard of this. In fact, I wasn't sure my father knew that Rolf and my mother had married until he stepped into the courtroom. Maybe she had sent him a postcard or something. He certainly hadn't been invited to the wedding.

"Why do you want to do this?" the judge asked.

"Peak is my son. It's time I stepped forward and took some responsibility."

I looked at my mother and Rolf. They were both staring straight ahead, expressionless.

"What do you think?" the judge asked.

Traci elbowed me in the side and I turned back around. "Me?"

The judge nodded.

"Uh . . . that would be great . . . uh . . . Your Honor."

The judge turned his attention back to my father. "Do you have the wherewithal to support and raise a fourteen-year-old boy?"

"We've prepared a complete financial statement," Traci said. She grabbed a sheaf of papers from the desk and took it up to the bench.

The judge flipped through the pages.

"As you can see, Mr. Wood is a very successful businessman."

"On paper," the judge said begrudgingly. He looked at my father again. "Where do you live, Mr. Wood?"

"Chiang Mai," my father answered.

"What state's that in?"

"It's in Thailand."

This was followed by a very long silence, and I felt the drain plug loosen.

"What about Peak's schooling?" the judge finally asked.

"There's an International School less than five miles from my house," my father answered. "I've already enrolled him. He'll begin in August."

"Peak is currently attending the Greene Street School," Traci said. "He only has one requirement left to complete this year. It should be easily accomplished in Thailand."

"The Greene Street School?" The judge smiled for the first time. "It just so happens that I went to GSS when I was a kid."

I didn't know they had legal prodigies.

The judge waved the prosecutor up to the bench, where they had a long whispered conversation. When it was over he looked at all of us one by one.

"All right," he said. "This is what we're going to do. Peak, you are on probation until you reach the age of eighteen. If, during that time, you break a law in the state of New York, thus violating your probation, you will immediately serve out the rest of your time in a juvenile detention facility. Do you understand?"

"Yes."

"Furthermore, the court fines you one hundred fifty thousand dollars . . ."

My shock must have shown, because the judge put up his hand for me to calm down.

"The money will be held in escrow by the state and returned if you fulfill the terms of your probation." He looked over at my three parents. "I assume you can scrape the money together."

"No problem, Your Honor," my father said. Mom and Rolf concurred.

"If I'm going to cut Peak loose, we have to make this look good," the judge continued. "I'm putting a gag order on all of you. You are not to discuss any aspect of this case with the media or anyone else. Especially the refundable fine. We want to discourage people from copying Peak's idiotic stunt. In other words, we want this to go away."

He looked at Traci and me.

"Poof!" he said.

THE TWINS

THE JUDGE TOLD US there was a swarm of reporters waiting in front of JDC and we would have to leave the back way.

My father was the first to go. He said he had some errands to run and he would meet me at the airport. It occurred to me that I should thank him, but by then, he was halfway down the hallway, tearing the tie off his neck like it was an anaconda. I guessed I would have plenty of time to thank him later, since we were going to be spending the next three years together.

Mom gave me my passport and a small backpack stuffed with clothes. Rolf had gone off to find the twins.

"Are you coming to the airport?" I asked, still feeling a little numb.

"Of course," she said. "But we may not have time to wait for your flight to leave. Rolf has a trial."

I flipped through the pages of the passport. "So, you knew I was leaving?"

"Not really," she answered. "Josh got in late yesterday, and we spent the whole night trying to put this together."

"Are you okay with this?"

"I don't know," she said. "It would have been nice to plan it out a bit more, but Josh has to get back. It's probably just as well. I think the thing that tipped it for the judge was the fact that you would be gone today."

"Poof," I said.

She smiled. "And we can get you back as fast as you disappeared." She pulled out a credit card and an international calling card from her purse and gave them to me. "If things go sour, or you just want to come home, use these."

I slipped the cards into the pocket of one of the Moleskines in my backpack.

"Once you get there, we'll ship whatever clothes you want."

"How long?" I asked.

"That's up to you, I guess. If you make it to the end of summer, we'll reevaluate. But if you want to come back sooner all you have to do is call. The judge didn't put any restrictions on when you could come back."

"What about Dad?" I asked. "I mean—"

"I know exactly what you mean," she said. "Josh seems to have mellowed since the last time we saw him. He traveled a long way to help. I can't tell you how shocked I was when he stepped into Traci's office. At that point we were absolutely desperate. The best Traci thought she could do was get a reduced sentence. Josh listened to the situation, then proceeded to outline exactly what happened today in the courtroom. When you're at the end of your rope there's no one better than Joshua Wood. Unfortunately, he doesn't pay much attention until you're dangling." She laughed. "Rolf and Traci said he should have become an attorney instead of a mountain climber."

"I'd better go talk to the twins," I said.

AS SOON AS ROLF and Mom left us alone, Patrice and Paula burst into tears.

"Who's going to walk us to school?"

"Who's going to walk us home?"

"Who's going to play with us at the park?"

"What about our birthday?"

"Why did you have to climb that stupid building, anyway?"

It was easy to become confused around the two Peas. They had a mysterious way of looking at things. They also tended to finish each other's sentences as if they shared the same brain.

I guess I should explain our relationship. They were born on my eighth birthday, which at first did not go over very well with me. You don't want to spend your eighth birthday in a loft with a babysitter while your mother and nervous stepfather are at the hospital having twins. From then on *your* special day is going to be the twins' special day, too. It took me a good two years, but the twins finally won me over. They were brilliant, hilarious little Peas and worshipped the ground I walked on (which really helped). They had a full-time nanny for the first few years, but I started spending so much time with them, Mom and Rolf let her go. Paula and Patrice were probably the best birthday presents I could have ever gotten.

And for the first time since I'd gotten busted, I really regretted climbing that stupid skyscraper. What was I going to do without the two Peas?

"We read that your daddy is not the same as our daddy." Patrice sniffled.

I cringed. Another terrible result from the moron climbing the skyscraper.

We had never told them that I was their half brother. Rolf

and Mom thought it would just confuse them. (They always underestimated the twins.) But I hadn't wanted them to learn about it from the newspaper. It hadn't taken the reporters long to figure out Spider Boy was Joshua Wood's son.

"We're half sisters," Patrice said.

Paula shook her head and rolled her eyes. "I already explained that to you. One half plus one half equals one. That's a whole. Together we are his whole sister."

"That's right," Patrice said. "I forgot."

(I told you they had a mysterious way of looking at things.)

"We always wondered why your last name was different from our last name," Paula said. "I thought it was because we were twins and you weren't. Some kind of name rule."

When Mom and Rolf got married I kept Mom's maiden name, Marcello. Rolf offered to adopt me legally, but I passed. I liked my last name and didn't want to change it. And I didn't like Rolf all that much. (There was nothing the matter with him, really. It's just that he wasn't my real father. More on that later.)

"You're going to Thailand," Patrice said. "Where they make these." She pulled on my necktie.

"Not quite," I said. "Thailand is a country in Southeast Asia, just south of China."

"When will you come back?" Paula asked.

"I'm not sure," I said.

"Will you be here for our birthday?"

"Birth*days,*" Patrice corrected.

"Will you?"

"I hope so," I said. "But it costs a lot of money to fly from Thailand to New York."

"We have money."

"Sixty-four dollars and thirty-five cents."

Paula shook her head. "Sixty-four dollars and forty-seven cents."

"Is that enough?"

"Maybe," I said. "Look, I'm going to miss you, and I want you to write me a lot of letters."

"We promise," they said in unison.

Mom and Rolf came back into the room.

"We'd better get going," Rolf said.

ROLF PULLED UP to the departure curb at the airport and we all got out. Mom started crying, and when the twins saw her crying, they started crying.

I gave them a group hug. As I held them I glanced at Rolf. He was standing off to the side, awkwardly as usual, and I realized that I was going to miss him, too. I gently untangled myself from the girls and walked over to him.

"I'm sorry about all the trouble," I said.

Rolf put his hand on my shoulder and smiled. "It's going to be pretty boring without you around. Take care of yourself and don't hesitate to use those cards." He looked at Mom and the twins, and for the first time ever I saw tears in his eyes. "We're going to miss you."

ROCK RATS

MY DAD WASN'T at the airline counter when I got to the airport. Our flight wasn't scheduled to take off for another three hours, so I wasn't worried . . . yet.

I went into the restroom and discovered Mom had filled my pack with all the clothes she liked (not necessarily my favorites), but they were better than the suit, which I stuffed into a garbage can. It was too small for me, anyway.

Two hours and fifty-five minutes to go. Waiting at an airport might be the worst . . . well, except for waiting in jail.

I bought an evil-looking hot dog and wolfed it down with a flat soda.

Two hours and fifty-three minutes.

I went through my pack and found the two Moleskines, and I thought about starting my assignment. All I had to do was fill one of them, but at that point I had no idea what I was going to write about.

I found an automatic pencil in an airport store, but when I sat down and pulled the wrapping off, the eraser shot off into space, and I couldn't find it. I wrote: Moleskine #1 on the first page, then put the pencil and the Moleskine away.

Discouraging.

Two hours and thirty-seven minutes.

As I sat there watching everyone coming and going, it finally dawned on me that I was free, and this got me thinking about what had led up to this—and I don't mean climbing skyscrapers, or getting arrested, or the trial. I mean way back. Back before I was born . . .

I WAS CONCEIVED in a two-man tent under the shadow of El Capitan in Yosemite National Park.

At least that's when my mom thinks it happened.

My parents were twenty-four years old at the time. The day before the tent, they had reached the summit of El Cap along the Iron Hawk route in the record time of thirty-two hours and forty-three minutes. And this was not the only climbing record they had broken that year: Hallucinogen Wall, Body Wax, the Flingus Cling, and dozens of other records had fallen to the climbing team of Teri Marcello and Joshua Wood.

Climbing magazines and equipment companies had started to pay attention to them . . . and to pay them money. The rusty old van they had lived in for three years was ditched for a brand-new four-wheel-drive truck camper. No more temp jobs to scrape together money for gas and food, no more mooching off the weekend climbers. They bought a piece of property in Wyoming and built a log cabin in front of a ninety-foot vertical wall, perfect for conditioning climbs. The rock rats were on their way up.

I'd seen photos of them back then. My father looked like a bodybuilder, but he was as flexible as a gymnast. My favorite photo of him was the one where he was standing on a high ledge touching his knees with his nose.

My mother was a foot shorter than my father. She was lean, with dreadlocks tickling her powerful shoulders, muscles in her arms and legs like knotted ropes, and abs like speed bumps. She was bulletproof.

But she was not baby proof.

Two months after El Cap she told my father she was pregnant. I have no idea what his reaction was, but I doubt he jumped up and down for joy when he got the good news.

It was a difficult pregnancy. There were complications. She was told to stay in bed or she would lose me. She did, but my father was on the move, teaching seminars, endorsing equipment, and climbing—shattering records on Mount Kilimanjaro, Mount McKinley, and Annapurna, which is where he was the night I was born.

He called her from Base Camp on a satellite phone after reaching the summit.

"What do you want to name him?" Mom asked.

"Peak."

"Pete?"

"No, Peak. P-E-A-K. Like 'mountain peak.'"

He didn't lay eyes on me until I was three months old, and that's when my mother had her accident in the backyard. I was there, strapped into a car seat at the base of the wall (and at that age, probably staring at the prairie dogs popping out of their holes, only dimly aware that I had parents at all).

They were thirty feet up the wall, free-climbing. For rock rats like them, this was like strolling across a level parking lot. Mom reached up and grabbed a handful of rotten rock. It was still clutched in her hand when my dad got down to her, which was probably five seconds after she hit the ground.

Thirty feet. Shattered hip. Broken back.

My dad canceled all his seminars, climbs, everything,

staying right at her side through the whole orthopedic jigsaw puzzle. It took nearly a year to put her back together. Wheelchair, crutches, and finally, when she was able to hobble around with a cane, Dad left again, showing up a couple times a year for a day or two at a time.

It took Mom two more years of physical therapy to ditch the cane, but she never climbed again.

Dad took me climbing for the first time when I was five years old. (We tried to keep it a secret, but the fly rods and fishing gear didn't fool Mom for one minute.) Only four more climbs with him over the next two years, but in between I made hundreds of solo ascents on the wall in back of the cabin with Mom manning the belay rope, shouting instructions up to me.

Then Rolf showed up on our doorstep. The New York lawyer in shining armor. He and Mom had actually grown up together in Nebraska. Neighbors. Rolf had been smitten with her since they were eight years old. After high school, Mom hit the road to climb rocks. Rolf went to Harvard to study law.

He arrived at the cabin at night in the middle of a blizzard. We were sitting in front of the woodstove reading. (We didn't have a television back then.) There was a knock on the door (actually more like a desperate banging), jolting both of us from our books. Our cabin was sixteen miles from the nearest town. People didn't drop by at ten o'clock at night (except for Dad, who never announced his arrivals and wouldn't think about knocking).

Mom opened the front door and there stood Rolf, although she didn't recognize him at first. He wasn't dressed for a Wyoming winter. He had on a light jacket, khaki pants, and tennis shoes. He was trying to control it, but his teeth were chattering. There was a quiver in his voice, which could have been from the cold, but I think it was more from fear. It had been over ten years since he had seen my mother.

"Hi, Teri," he said.

"Rolf?"

"Yeah . . . uh . . . my rental car kind of slid off the road a mile back or so. I would have called, but you're not listed."

"We use a cell phone out here. It's just easi— Well, never mind that . . ." She pulled him inside and made him a cup of hot chocolate, then gave him some of my dad's clothes, which were too big for him.

I went to bed, so I don't know what happened that first night, but he became a regular guest at the cabin for the next several months, flying in for long weekends whenever he could. Rolf made my mom laugh and I liked him for that, but aside from that we didn't have much in common. I guess I resented him for horning in on the simple life we had made in the wilderness.

He took us to New York, which was interesting, but noisy and confusing compared to the prairie. At the end of our two-week stay, they sat me down in Rolf's kitchen and told me they were going to get married.

"Okay," I said, not really knowing what that meant at the time.

I later learned that it meant we were selling the cabin in Wyoming and moving to the loft in New York. It meant that my real dad would no longer be popping in for visits. It meant the Greene Street School. It meant that the closest I was going to get to a rock wall for the next few years was the fifteen-footer at the YMCA down the street, which I could have climbed backward without protection if the guys manning the ropes would have allowed it. None of this helped to sweeten my relationship with Rolf.

The twins saved me. And it also helped that my mom let me subscribe to a half dozen climbing magazines. In the back of one of those magazines I discovered summer climbing camps. It took a lot of sulking to get her to let me go to one of them. What cinched it in the end was that she knew the climbing instructor. A former rock rat gone legit.

After this, as long as I did well in school, she let me sign up for more camps.

Then the time lag between the climbs became a problem. I started eyeing skyscrapers, telling myself that I would just *plan* the route up but not climb it. Right.

To get up a rock wall you study the outside, trying to pick the best footholds and handholds, guessing where you're going to encounter problems so you have the right equipment with you to get around them.

To climb a skyscraper you have to know the inside as well as the outside. (Which is where I screwed up on my last climb.) You don't want to be dangling outside of a window when someone is at a desk working or vacuuming the floor.

You also have to plan your exits. Mine were pretty simple. I used the elevators.

Rooftops have doors. Late on the day of the climb, while the building was still open, I'd go up to the roof and put a piece of duct tape over the latch. After I climbed to the top I'd slip into the stairwell and spend the night. In the morning, when the building started to fill up with workers, I'd walk down a few floors, get on an elevator, punch the lobby button, and walk out as if I had just finished an early dentist or doctor's appointment, getting home before Mom, Rolf, or the twins knew I was gone.

I guess my plan didn't quite work out in the Woolworth Building.

BANGKOK

ONE HOUR AND FORTY-THREE MINUTES.

And still no sign of my father.

I had made one trip out of the country with Rolf, Mom, and the twins (London, two summers ago) and knew that you had to check in early for international flights.

Where was he? What kind of errands was he running? What if he didn't show? (And all the other boring questions that run through your mind when you're waiting.)

I walked over to the flight information monitor, thinking that maybe our flight was delayed. ON TIME, it read.

Above the monitor was a regular TV. I glanced at it, and was going to turn away until the anchor said: "The state of New York has reached a plea agreement with Peak Marcello, the boy who climbed the Woolworth Building early last week. He was sentenced to three years of probation and fined a whopping one hundred fifty thousand dollars! This is the steepest penalty ever given for criminal trespass in New York's history . . ."

The camera cut to a shot of the mayor getting into the back of a black limo. He turned to the reporter and said: "This should put an end to people climbing skyscrapers in the city of New York. This illegal activity will no longer be tolerated under any circumstances."

"Peak Marcello and his family were unavailable for comment," said the reporter, "and it is believed the boy has left the state of New York for an undisclosed location."

Not yet, I thought, turning away, grateful they hadn't run a photo of me.

"Peak!"

Finally. My father was pushing a huge cart with a mountain of gear piled on it. I trotted over.

"Give me a hand."

I helped him push the cart up to the counter. "What is all this stuff?"

"I don't get to New York very often and thought I should stock up on some supplies. Give me your passport."

He put it down on the counter along with his own battered passport, which looked like it had been through the wash a couple times.

"You're cutting it a little close, Mr. Wood," the attendant said.

"I know," my father said. "Family emergency."

The attendant pointed at the cart. "This exceeds your baggage limit."

My father took a credit card out of his pocket. "Just put it on this."

By the time we had everything checked we had only minutes to catch the flight. We were the last ones down the Jetway.

"I couldn't get us seats together," he said as we stepped onto the airplane. "But at least we're both in business class." He pointed out my seat, then took his own, which was three rows behind me, and that's the last time I talked to him for thirteen hours.

We had a three-hour layover at the Narita airport near Tokyo, but I didn't get a chance to talk to him there, either, because he spent the entire time on his cell phone speaking in what sounded like Chinese, but it could have been Thai or Nepalese, as far as I knew. He was still jabbering on the phone when we boarded the plane for Bangkok, where I was disappointed again to see that we were in separate rows.

Another six hours passed.

On the way to customs in Bangkok, I finally caught him between calls.

"I'm really sorry about all this, Dad. You having to come all the way to the States, the money, being stuck with me—"

"Whoa," he said, holding up his calloused climbing hand. "First, you don't have to call me Dad. I don't deserve the title. For the time being, let's pretend I'm your big brother. Just call me Josh like all my friends do. Second, don't worry about the money. Rolf and your mom put a big chunk of change in. I'll get my portion back. And finally, I'm not stuck with you. I couldn't be happier to have you with me. I just haven't had much time to show it because I'm trying to put something together."

"What?" I asked.

"A surprise, but in the meantime, no worries."

We continued down toward customs, where there was another little problem. I didn't have a visa to enter Thailand. ~~My father~~ Josh took my passport and disappeared into a room with a couple customs officers and came back out ten minutes later.

"We're in the clear," he said, hurrying through the airport toward the terminal, bypassing baggage claim.

"What about your gear?"

"We'll get it tomorrow. No worries."

Outside we climbed into the back of a cab.

"We're not going to Chiang Mai?"

"Not yet. We'll get there eventually."

It was well after midnight, but Bangkok was wide awake. The cabbie crazily swerved between bicycles, motorcycles, and cars for twenty minutes, finally coming to a stop in front of a hotel.

Josh paid the driver and we walked into the lobby, where the concierge beamed at us.

"Mr. Wood, I have your rooms all ready."

He handed each of us a key.

"Okay," Josh said as we got into the elevator, "I have some more errands to do tomorrow. In the morning I'll have a driver waiting for you in the lobby. Nine o'clock. He'll take you to the clinic for a physical."

"Physical?"

"Yeah . . . Uh . . . an immigration formality, and I want them to check your face and ear." He took my hands and looked at my damaged fingers. "We'll need to get those fixed, too. Anyway, I'll come by the clinic and pick you up when you're finished, and we'll be on our way. If I'm late, just wait for me there. Try to get some sleep. I don't want you to flunk the physical because you're tired."

WHEN I WOKE UP I didn't even know what day it was. Couldn't remember if you lost a day or gained a day in Thailand. I ate breakfast, went for a walk, and got back to the hotel and waited for my driver.

The clinic turned out to be a huge hospital and it took a while for me and the driver to find Dr. Woo's office. He was expecting me. In fact, it turned out I was the only patient he had that day.

I'd had physicals before, but nothing like this. Dr. Woo and his nurse didn't speak English, so they had to pantomime me through the battery of tests. I was X-rayed, CAT-scanned, and jabbed with countless needles. They put me on treadmills and stationary bicycles with so many leads attached to my body and tubes jammed in my mouth, I wouldn't have been able to ask them what they were doing even if I spoke Thai. They must have drawn a quart of blood over the course of the day. They checked my eyes, ears, mouth, and other holes I don't even want to think about. They took the stitches out of my ear. Another doctor came in and looked at my feet, knees, shoulders, hips, elbows, wrists, and finally my fingers, which he put some salve on and bandaged, then gave me instructions on how to do it myself, which I barely understood. By the time they finished with me, it was late afternoon, and I was so exhausted I wanted to check myself into the hospital as a patient.

The nurse led me to the waiting room and I promptly fell asleep on an uncomfortable chair. And that's where Josh woke me sometime after dark. Apparently, he had been there for a while talking to Dr. Woo because he had a thick file in his hand, which I assumed were Dr. Woo's findings.

"Am I going to live?" I asked groggily.

"No worries," Josh said. "I'm not surprised you're in such great shape with my and your mother's genes. Let's go; we have an airplane to catch."

I was looking forward to Chiang Mai, where I could finally get some rest.

His gear was waiting for him outside the airport, guarded

by a porter the size of a sumo wrestler. He paid the porter, wheeled the cart to the counter, and said, "We're booked on the flight to Kathmandu."

I wasn't sure I had heard him right.

"Did you say Kathmandu?"

"Right."

"I thought we were going to Chiang Mai."

"We will," he said as he transferred gear to the conveyor belt. "But we have a stop to make first."

He must have bought the gear for someone in Kathmandu.

"Actually, a couple of stops," he added as he threw on the last box.

"Where's the second stop?" I asked.

"Everest," he said.

I stared at him. For a climber, saying that you are stopping by Everest is like saying you're going to stop by and see God.

Josh was grinning at me. "I didn't want to tell you until I had it all worked out. Your physical was the last hurdle, that and the Chinese visa."

"Kathmandu is in Nepal," I pointed out.

"Right," Josh said. "But we're not going up the south side in Nepal. We're going up the north side in Tibet. You have to be sixteen to get a permit to go up the Nepalese side. The Chinese aren't quite so picky. They don't care how old you are as long as you pay the fee. And then there are the twenty-five clients I have waiting at—"

"I'm climbing Everest?" I asked, more stunned than I've ever been in my life.

"I don't know if you'll make the summit," he said. "But if

we get you up there before your fifteenth birthday you'll be the youngest person in the world ever to stand above twenty-nine thousand feet." He picked up the tickets and started toward the gate.

I followed him numbly. He didn't have to ask if I wanted to go. Every climber in the world wants to summit Everest, or at least give it a try.

On the airplane Josh waved me into the window seat and sat down in the seat next to mine. The plane backed away from the Jetway.

"Does Mom know about this?" I asked.

"Uh . . . no, but I'll give her a call. No worries."

THE SUMMIT HOTEL

WHEN THE MESSAGE about my arrest reached Josh he had been in Tibet on his way to Base Camp on the north side of Everest. With him were twenty-five clients, fifteen Sherpas, and about fifty porters and their yaks.

Twelve of the clients were trying for the summit, the other thirteen had signed up for one of the four lower camps along the northern route. The higher you climbed, the more it cost.

"I caught a truck heading back to Kathmandu and sent the others on to Base Camp," he explained. "That's why I've been rushing around. I don't want to lose my acclimatization, and I need to get back to my clients. They weren't too happy about me abandoning them on the way to the mountain."

"Thanks again for bailing me out," I said.

"Forget it," he said, leaning his seat back and pulling his cap over his eyes. Within a minute he was sound asleep.

Why had he done it? That was the question bouncing around in my jet-lagged brain. He was my father, but that was a technicality more than a fact.

I had written him at least a dozen letters over the years, but I had never gotten a letter (or even a postcard) in return. Mom said that Josh wasn't much for letter writing, and that there was a good chance he never got my letters. There weren't too many post offices in the places he hung out.

So why, after all these years, did he show up? Guilt? Not likely. That emotion didn't seem to fit him. My mother told me once that Josh always slept like a baby because he had no conscience to keep him awake. He was demonstrating that right now, quietly snoring as we winged our way to Kathmandu.

KATHMANDU. For me the name conjured up mystery, adventure, possibilities, but the reality was somewhat different. The city is noisy, grimy, and polluted. My eyes burned and I started choking as soon as we stepped outside the airport.

"Takes some getting used to," Josh said as our taxi sputtered into an unbroken line of traffic. "You'll be staying at the Summit Hotel."

"Me?"

"Just for a couple days," Josh said. "I need to get up to Base Camp before there's a revolt. I don't have time to stay with you while you acclimatize, and you need to acclimatize slowly. You know the routine."

I did know the routine. I'd read at least a dozen books about conquering 8,000-meter peaks (peaks above 26,000 feet), including the three books my father had written. There are fourteen of these peaks in the world.

It can take at least two months to get to the top of Everest, which is actually 8,850 meters tall. The long climbing time is not because of the distance, which is less than five miles, but because it's up.

Most of the climbing time is spent sitting in the six camps along the route, letting your body get used to the thin air. If you go up too fast you might get mountain sickness, or high altitude pulmonary edema (HAPE). Here's how HAPE works: Your lungs fill with fluid, you can't breathe, you go into a coma, then you die.

The only way to treat HAPE is to get to a lower altitude where there's more oxygen (or "Os," as climbers call it). It doesn't matter what kind of physical condition you're in. If you climb up faster than your body can adjust, you'll get HAPE and your climb is over—maybe forever. The only chance you have of reaching the top of Everest (or any 8,000-meter peak) is to "climb high, sleep low" until your body is ready to make the push to the summit. In other words, you have to make sure your lungs keep up with your legs—it's a very bad idea to leave your lungs behind.

The other problem with Everest is that there is only a small window when the weather is good enough to get to the top. Two weeks, maybe less. (Some years, the window is only two days.) You have to be positioned in the right place, at the right time, in the right physical condition, or you'll never make it to the summit.

Because Josh has spent most of his life training and climbing at high altitudes he could almost jog up to Base Camp (18,000 feet). Well, not really, but he could certainly get up there in half the time it was going to take me coming from sea level in New York City. Without me he would be at Base Camp in four or five days. If he waited for my lungs to catch up with his it would take him ten days to two weeks to get to Base Camp.

What he hadn't explained was how I was going to get to Tibet on my own, and he didn't get a chance to tell me right then because the taxi had just pulled into the courtyard of the Summit Hotel, where we were immediately surrounded by a swarm of laughing, smiling Nepalese.

"Hotel staff," he said.

They obviously knew he was coming and were overjoyed that he was there. We got out and he introduced me. Not speaking Nepalese, I didn't know if he told them I was his son or his little brother. Regardless, by their expressions they were very happy to make my acquaintance.

They unloaded the gear and we followed them into the lobby, where we encountered more pandemonium—this time from the guests. Women, men, trekkers, mountain climbers, old and young, gathered around Josh like he was a rock star (no pun intended). He signed autographs and answered questions until the concierge, politely but firmly, dispersed the crowd.

"Please, please . . . Mr. Wood needs to rest after his long journey."

Mr. Wood had no intention of resting. When we got to the room he started sorting through the gear and stuffing what he wanted into his backpack.

"You're leaving now?" I asked, trying not to sound too whiny.

"Have to." The last thing he jammed into his pack was a box of energy bars.

I didn't say, "What about me?" because there is no way to say this without sounding pitiful, so I just stared at him.

"Zopa will be taking you up to Base Camp," he said. "Aside from myself, he's the only one I trust to do it. He knows all about you."

"Who's Zopa? And how does he know about me?"

He sat down on the edge of the bed. "Zopa used to be *sirdar.* You know what that is?"

"Head Sherpa," I said.

Sherpas are mountain people who live on the slopes of the Himalayas. Without them and their climbing skills, no one would get to the summit of Everest.

"Right," Josh said. "Zopa got me to the summit of Annapurna the day you were born. He was there when Teri called and gave me the news. Since then, he's asked me about you every time I've seen him. Bugging me, really . . . saying that it's not good for a father to neglect his son."

Obviously, Josh had not listened to him.

"Zopa stopped climbing years ago," he continued. "He's a Buddhist monk now. Lives at the Indrayani temple. The Lama there has given him permission to forgo his vows for a few weeks to take you up to Base Camp."

"Forgo his vows?"

"It's not as big a deal as it sounds. I don't know all the details, but leading you to Base Camp was considered to be auspicious, meaning the right thing to do." Josh smiled. "And I'm sure the donation I made to the temple didn't hurt. They're a little strapped for money."

"So, Zopa is okay with this?"

"Absolutely. He's curious about you. And he didn't say this, but I think he's getting kind of bored with being a monk."

"What's he like?"

"Cagey," Josh said with a smile. "If he agrees to do something, he'll do it, but he may not be doing it for the reason you think he's doing it. And he'll never let you in on why he's doing it."

"Huh?" Josh was beginning to sound like Paula and Patrice.

"It's hard to explain," he said. "You never know what

Zopa's real motivation is. I asked him to take you up to Base Camp. He said he would, but he's not taking you up there just to do me a favor or because I gave money to the temple. There's another reason—more likely half dozen reasons—he agreed to do it. And you and I will probably never know what all of them are.

"It was a sad day when he retired, I can tell you that. He's been on the summit of Everest more than any other human being. At least that's the rumor. Zopa says he can't remember how many times he's reached the top, but I think he knows exactly how many times it's been. He speaks perfect English, and although he doesn't talk very much, when he does you need to listen very carefully to what he's saying. The Sherpas do. A lot of them drop by the temple before they climb to have him do a reading. If he tells them not to go, they won't go up, no matter how much money we offer them."

"How do I get in touch with him?"

"He'll come by in a day or two. In the meantime, you need to sort through this gear. Most of it's yours and you'll need all of it to get up the mountain. I wasn't sure on the sizes, but if something doesn't fit right tell Zopa and he'll swap it out at one of the shops downtown." He looked at his watch. "I'd better get going."

He started toward the door and stopped. "Charge whatever you eat at the restaurant to the room. Do you have any cash?"

I shook my head.

He pulled out a thick wad of money and peeled off several bills.

"It's not as much as it looks like. Seven thousand rupees is about a hundred and fifty bucks U.S."

I took the bills and set them on the dresser.

"I'll see you in a couple of weeks," Josh said. "Maybe less if Zopa thinks you're ready. Oh . . . Before I leave town I'll call your mom and tell her you're okay."

I interpreted this to mean that he would call and lie to her about where we were and what we were doing. Better him than me.

"Enjoy the trip," he said, and with this he was gone.

I stood there for a few seconds, staring at the door. My head was kind of spinning, but it wasn't from altitude. I think it was Josh's energy that was making me dizzy.

There was a light tapping on the door, so faint I barely heard it. I opened it.

It was the concierge. He gave me a slight bow.

"I will turn down your bed."

He wove his way through the junk as if it weren't there, pulled the comforter back, and fluffed the pillows. When he finished he looked at the window. The curtains were drawn.

"This will not do!" he said. "You are missing the setting of the sun."

He pulled the curtains back with a flourish.

Behind them were the Himalayas washed in orange and pink light. They were much bigger than I had ever imagined.

GEAR OF THE DEAD

THE NEXT MORNING, after a huge breakfast in the dining room, I came back upstairs and started sorting through the gear.

All the stuff didn't make up for all the birthdays and Christmases Josh had neglected, but it came pretty darn close. It was all state-of-the-art equipment, most of which I'd only seen advertised in climbing magazines. Camp stove, coils of rope, cams, titanium ice ax, crampons, thermal gloves, digital camera, O_2 regulator and face mask, tent, subzero sleeping bag, sleeping pad, altimeter watch, carabiners, batteries, ascenders, pitons, harnesses, climbing helmet, headlamp . . . Everything I needed to get through the death zone.

Most of the clothes were too small, especially the boots. I suppose Josh couldn't have asked my mother for my sizes without tipping her off. And he couldn't have asked me, because until I passed the physical he wasn't sure I was going, which got me to wondering what he would have done if I had failed the physical.

But only for a moment.

The gear called to me, and nothing matters when you are up to your knees in brand-new, expensive climbing equipment.

It took me two hours to figure out how the altimeter watch worked. An hour to set up the tent. I faced it with the opening toward the window so I could see the Himalayas. I snapped a couple photos of my view with the digital camera, then I got hungry and decided rather than going down to the dining room I'd just cook up some food on my brand-new camp stove. (I know this sounds goofy, but I get a little out of control when it comes to gear. I opened the window so I didn't get carbon monoxide poisoning.)

As the freeze-dried beef Stroganoff was simmering away there was a knock on my door. I thought it was housekeeping again. They had come by earlier asking to clean the room, but I told them that I had everything I needed and to come back tomorrow. I slithered out of the tent, carefully stepped over the stove (so I didn't tip it over and burn down the hotel), and cracked open the door, hoping they wouldn't smell the gas burning or the food cooking.

It wasn't the housekeeper. It was a Nepalese boy, about my age but two inches shorter. He was smiling up at my head, which is all I had revealed through the crack. Below my head I had nothing on but my boxers because I had been trying on gear all day and it was getting hot in the room from the stove and the sun coming through the window.

"Peak Wood?" he asked.

"Actually, it's Peak Marcello, but yeah, that's me."

"My name is Sun-jo. Zopa sent me over to bring you to him."

"Oh sure . . . uh . . ." I glanced at the mess behind me. I didn't want to leave him standing in the hallway while I got ready, which was going to take a while.

Appearing like a total idiot won over being rude. I let him in.

Sun-jo looked a bit shocked at the setup, but he didn't burst out laughing, which I might have done if I had stumbled onto something equally as stupid-looking as my indoor camp spot.

"My dad . . . uh, I mean Josh, got me some new gear and I was . . . uh . . . testing it out, so I would know . . ." *Ah, forget it,* I thought. "I'm just making some lunch. Are you hungry?"

Sun-jo said he was.

As I got dressed, I watched him checking out the equipment, and I knew he was a climber. No one else would fondle gear as lovingly. He picked up various items like they were more valuable than gold, which they *were* when they were the only thing keeping you from falling off a rock face or into a dark bottomless crevasse.

I cleared a spot for us on the bed and served him a bowl of Stroganoff and an energy bar for dessert. It turned out that Sun-jo's father had been a Sherpa. Unfortunately, he had died up on K2 the previous year trying to rescue a group of climbers. Only one of the climbers survived.

K2 was discovered in 1856 by a surveyor named T. G. Montgomery. The *K* stands for Karakoram. The *2* means it was the second peak Montgomery listed on his survey. At 28,250 feet it's a bit shorter than Everest, but most climbers agree it's a lot harder to reach the summit.

I told Sun-jo how sorry I was to hear about his father, but he shrugged it off, saying he hardly knew his dad. He and his two younger sisters had spent most of their lives at a private boarding school in northern India.

"My sisters and I only came back to Kathmandu on holiday," he said. "My father was usually up on the mountain during those times."

Hearing about his sisters caused a little ache in my belly for Paula and Patrice, but it went away as I watched Sun-jo casually tie a length of Spectra cord to a hex slung with a triple fisherman's knot.

"Where did you learn to climb?" I asked.

"My grandfather instructed me," he answered.

His English was better than mine. He had kind of a British/Indian accent. Mine was kind of a Bronx/Cody, Wyoming, accent—which did not sound nearly as cool or refined as his.

"So, you're on holiday?"

"No," Sun-jo answered. "When my father died we did not have the funds to keep all three of us in school. The tuition is very expensive. My sisters are still in school and I am here to find work so they can stay there. Without a formal education there is no future for girls in Kathmandu. I would like to go back to school myself, but it is unlikely I will be able to. It is more important that my sisters attend school than it is for me."

Sun-jo wasn't much older than I was, and I wondered what kind of job he could get that would pay the tuition.

He looked at my altimeter watch, which he had been playing with throughout lunch. "We should leave soon. Zopa is waiting for us at the Indrayani temple."

I turned off the stove and put the dishes in the bathroom sink.

"Did you know there is a dining room here in the hotel?" Sun-jo asked. "I have not dined there myself, but I hear it is quite excellent."

"Yeah, I ate there this morning. It's great. The reason I cooked . . . well, you know . . . the new gear . . ."

Sun-jo smiled. He knew exactly what I was talking about.

OUR TRANSPORTATION to the temple was the saddest motorcycle I had ever seen. There was more silver duct tape on it than chrome.

It took him six vicious kicks to get it started, and when it finally caught, the motorcycle belched out a column of gray smoke so thick I thought the bike had burst into flames along with my new friend. But the smoke cleared, revealing a coughing Sun-jo with tears running down his face and a mostly intact motorcycle—except for the bolt lying in a pool of oil under the engine.

"It is much better when we are moving forward." He gasped. "In this way the smoke cannot catch us."

I thought about running up to the room and grabbing my climbing helmet, but I was afraid Sun-jo might die of asphyxiation before I got back out, so I climbed on behind him and we lurched into traffic.

Sun-jo yelled something that sounded like, "Only two root beers, last go!" But I think he meant that the motorcycle only had two foot gears, fast and slow. He was right about our exhaust being behind us; the problem was that we were now speeding through everyone else's exhaust. For the next twenty minutes I squeezed shut my burning eyes and buried my face in his back, thereby missing most of Kathmandu.

"We have arrived," Sun-jo announced.

I unclutched my sweaty hands and opened my eyes.

"You must remove your shoes before entering the temple."

I took them off and put them next to about fifty other pairs of shoes and sandals.

"If you don't mind my asking," Sun-jo said, "what happened to your face?"

"It got frozen to a building."

Sun-jo laughed. "No, really . . ."

"Climbing accident," I said.

"That's what I thought."

I followed him into the Indrayani temple, which was like walking into another world. One where people whispered rather than shouted. There were no wandering cows (we had narrowly missed three of them on the way over), no horns honking, no screeching tires. The smell of flowers and incense saturated the air. Worshippers were kneeling in front of shrines, spinning prayer wheels, lighting butter lamps. Mystery, possibilities—this was the Kathmandu I had expected.

Sun-jo led me to a teak bench in the shade of a banyan tree. We sat for a while watching the orange-robed monks talking quietly to visitors and offering them blessings.

"Which one is Zopa?" I whispered.

"None of these."

"Shouldn't we let him know we're here?"

Sun-jo shook his head. "He'll be along when he's ready."

Waiting again, but I didn't mind. I spent the time trying to figure out how to gracefully bow out of a return trip to the hotel on the death motorcycle.

"Here he comes," Sun-jo said.

I expected Zopa to be a frail old holy man. And the monk striding toward us was old, but he was anything but frail. His arm and calf muscles (what I could see of them beneath the hem of his orange robe) were well defined and powerful.

You'd expect a Buddhist monk to have a spiritual presence, but whatever spirituality Zopa had was overwhelmed by his physical presence. When he reached us he put his palms together and bowed. I followed Sun-jo's lead by getting to my feet and returning the bow.

Zopa looked me over, frowning at the scabs on my face and ear.

"Climbing accident," Sun-jo explained.

Zopa pointed at my bandaged fingers.

"Split nails," I explained nervously. "They're almost healed."

"You look like your father," Zopa said.

Actually, I looked more like my mother, but I wasn't about to disagree with him.

"How did you get here?"

"Motorcycle," Sun-jo said.

Zopa shook his head in disgust. "When you go back take a taxi." He reached into a fold in his robe and came out with a roll of rupees as big as his fist.

I didn't think Buddhist monks were even supposed to look at money.

He peeled off half an inch of bills and handed them to Sun-jo.

"What about my motorcycle?" Sun-jo asked.

"If you are lucky," Zopa said, "someone will steal it. Wait for me at the hotel."

The monk turned and walked away. I was relieved about the taxi, but that didn't explain why we had come all the way down to the Indrayani temple. When I asked Sun-jo about it he just shrugged and said that Zopa had his own way of doing things.

Mysterious ways, as it turned out, because when we got back to the hotel, Zopa was already waiting for us in the lobby. I didn't recognize him at first because the orange robe had been replaced by regular street clothes and an expensive-looking pair of sunglasses. The sunglasses made him look like some kind of celebrity, which I suppose he was to the trekkers and climbers gathered around him. It had taken us ten minutes tops to catch a taxi outside of the temple. We drove straight to the hotel, and traffic wasn't any worse than it had been on the motorcycle on the way to the temple. And yet, there was Zopa chatting with the hotel staff and guests as if he had been there all afternoon.

I looked at Sun-jo, expecting him to be as shocked as I was. He wasn't.

"Zopa does things like that," he said.

"How?"

Another shrug, which I learned later was everyone's answer to questions about Zopa.

"You'll get used to it," Sun-jo added, then went over and greeted the vacationing monk.

Now, you're probably wondering why I didn't ask Zopa myself. Believe me I was tempted, but I didn't think he would tell me. Or worse, he might give me some reasonable explanation. It's sort of like asking a magician to tell you how he does a trick. Or asking a tagger how he got those seventeen freight cars painted in a single night. It's all about the mystery. Sometimes it's better not to ask.

Up in the room, Zopa sorted through the gear, putting it in different piles while Sun-jo and I watched. Once in a while he would stop and have me try something on saying, "Fits," or "Doesn't fit." When he was finished there were three piles.

He pointed to one of the piles. “We will take this and trade for things that fit.”

My boots, blue snowsuit, and several other items of clothing were in a separate pile with some other stuff. I pointed out that none of the things in that pile fit, either.

“I have another use for it,” Zopa said.

I didn’t know what that could be, but I didn’t pursue it. Instead I pointed to the trade pile, which had several hundred dollars’ worth of pitons, cams, ropes, and other expensive equipment.

“This gear is brand-new,” I said.

“You won’t need it to get up Sagarmatha.”

This is what the Nepalese call Everest.

“My dad bought it,” I argued. “He might need it.”

“Your father told me to make sure that you have everything you need to climb the mountain. How much money do you have?”

I told him, but I didn’t mention the credit card Mom had given me. I didn’t think she’d be happy about a huge bill for Everest gear.

“It’s not enough to get the things you will need,” Zopa said. “Hopefully, we will be able to trade all this.” He started to gather up the gear from the trade pile.

“Best not to argue,” Sun-jo whispered, and he and I helped haul the gear downstairs, where a Toyota truck and driver were waiting for us.

IT TOOK HOURS to get the replacement gear. In the process I got quite a tour of Kathmandu. It seemed that most of the places Zopa liked to shop were located down dark scary alleys. He was warmly greeted wherever we went, until the bartering started, when he and the proprietor would end up in a shouting match until a bargain was struck.

The most difficult things to find were my boots. I'd try on a pair I liked, tell Zopa they fit great, then he would make me walk, and shake his head.

"Not right," he'd say.

"What do you mean?" I'd insist. "They fit great."

"Too small," he'd say. "But when your toes fall off inside from the swelling and pinching they will fit perfectly."

We finally agreed on a pair that did fit great, but they were pretty battered up on the outside. In fact, all the stuff we bought was banged up.

"I hope this gear wasn't taken from dead climbers," I said offhandedly.

Zopa looked horrified. "Bad luck to use gear of the dead. No, this is from people who come to Kathmandu to climb and decide it is better to stay in bar and drink."

I must have looked horrified myself.

"Don't think ill of them," he said. "They lived."

Zopa also bought a few things for himself and Sun-jo, who I guessed was coming with us to Base Camp by the gear he was getting. Unlike me, he listened carefully to Zopa's opinions and bowed every time the monk gave him something.

It was late when we got back to the hotel. We went up to the room, packed everything, then loaded it into the truck.

"We leave for Tibet tomorrow morning at six," Zopa said.

He and Sun-jo got into the truck and drove away.

TIBET

THE NEXT MORNING Sun-jo, Zopa, the driver, and two Sherpas were sitting on the tailgate drinking tea. By the look of their disheveled hair and rumpled clothes they must have slept in the truck.

Sun-jo confirmed that they had. "But only for two hours," he said. "We were out getting supplies up until then."

He wasn't kidding. There was so much stuff piled in the bed, I didn't know where we were going to sit.

We squeezed ourselves between the gear along with two Sherpas (brothers, named Yogi and Yash) and left the blue haze of Kathmandu behind us.

WE TOOK OUR TIME, stopping at Buddhist temples and monasteries along the way, where Zopa picked up boxes of food and supplies. We already had plenty of food and some of the food he was given wasn't going to last very long up on the mountain. I asked about it but got the standard shrug in reply.

Away from the city, Nepal was everything I had imagined it to be. Beautiful valleys, rustic villages, fields tilled by oxen-pulled plows, all against the backdrop of the massive, sparkling Himalayas. I had been up on Mount McKinley and Mount Rainier, but they would be dwarfed by these snow-covered peaks.

We stopped for the night outside a tiny village. Sun-jo and I started to help set up camp, but Zopa waved us off.

"You two go climb." He pointed to a wall about a quarter mile away. "Don't fall. Come down before dark."

He didn't have to tell us twice. We jogged over to the wall. It wasn't a difficult climb, but about halfway up I had to stop to rest and catch my breath. Sun-jo, who had picked a more difficult route, scrambled up the rock like a lizard, smiling as he climbed past, which taught me a couple of things about him. He had much better lung capacity than me—and he was competitive.

Climbers will tell you that the thing they love about climbing is that it's just them against the rock, blah, blah, blah. . . . That may be true if they are alone on the rock, but put another climber next to them, and the race is on.

I was shocked when he blew by me so effortlessly. I was the kid who was going to climb Everest, and Sun-jo was just along for the ride up to Base Camp. Then I reminded myself that ten days ago I was clinging to a skyscraper a few hundred feet above sea level—not exactly the best training for scaling the highest peak in the world. If I was going to summit I was going to have to do better than watch Sun-jo's butt disappear over the top as I hung below him gasping for breath.

"I think you picked the more difficult way," he said when I finally sat down next to him on the rim. We both knew this wasn't true, but I appreciated his saying it.

We sat on the edge for a while taking in the view. It was too late to climb down before dark, so we decided to rappel to the bottom. Sun-jo offered to let me go first, but I shook my head. First up, first down.

When we got back to camp dinner was ready. Zopa didn't say anything about the climb, but there was a spotting scope set up on a tripod pointed at the wall. He must have watched the whole thing.

The next morning Zopa told us the truck was overloaded and that Sun-jo and I would have to walk with our heavy packs.

"Why did Zopa do that?" Sun-jo complained as we watched the truck drive up the road. "The truck is fine. We haven't picked up more than fifty kilos of supplies."

I shrugged, but I thought I knew the answer. Zopa thought that a hike with a full pack would do me good and didn't want me to walk alone. Sorry, Sun-jo.

The walk was hard, but it was better than bouncing around in the back of a truck, and it gave Sun-jo and me a chance to get to know each other better.

Sun-jo's father didn't want him to become a Sherpa.

"The reason I climb," he had told him, "is so you won't have to."

"Does your mother know you're on your way to Base Camp?"

"No. And she would be very upset if she knew."

Later that day I spilled my guts about climbing the skyscraper, which I immediately regretted. When Sun-jo figured out that I was telling the truth, he stopped in the middle of the road and laughed for at least five minutes. It didn't seem that outrageous to me, but I guess to someone who lives in the shadow of the highest mountain in the world, climbing a skyscraper is pretty lame.

"Does your mother know you are on your way up to Sagarmatha?" he asked.

"I don't think so. And she would murder me and my father if she knew."

We finally caught up to the truck that evening. Zopa suggested we take another climb before we ate, but Sun-jo and I revolted and told him to forget it.

The next day he made us walk again.

HE GAVE US A BREAK on the fourth day because he wanted us all to cross into Tibet together.

We reached the Friendship Bridge about noon. I suppose if you're crossing south from Tibet into Nepal the name fits. But if you're going north from Nepal into Tibet there's nothing friendly about it.

The Chinese border soldiers were surly, suspicious, and rude. They examined our papers for nearly an hour and peppered us with questions I didn't understand. Zopa handled the answers calmly, but the rest of us were nervous—especially Sun-jo, who had started to sweat even though it was only thirty-five degrees.

"What's the matter with you?" I whispered.

"Nothing," he whispered back. "Chinese."

The soldiers nearly dismantled the truck looking for contraband. They didn't find any, but they did manage to steal some of our stuff in the process. Food mostly. But no one called them on it.

The day before, as we had walked, Sun-jo had given me a short history lesson about Tibet and China. It wasn't pretty. The People's Republic of China invaded Tibet fifty years ago. Since that time over six thousand Buddhist monasteries and shrines have been destroyed and hundreds of thousands of Tibetans have been killed or jailed.

Which brings me to that boulder in the middle of the road the prisoners were cracking into gravel. We passed by it an hour after we got over the Friendship Bridge, which sort of sums up what's happening to the Tibetans.

Or as Zopa put it later that night, "Our brothers in Tibet have been made slaves in their own country."

We stopped at every monastery that hadn't been burned to the ground or dismantled by the Chinese—some of them well out of our way. The monks were grateful for the food, supplies, and gossip Zopa and the Sherpas brought. It was clear that this was one of the half dozen reasons Zopa had for taking me to Base Camp.

Sun-jo and I hiked every day and climbed every evening. By the time we arrived at Base Camp ten days later I was feeling strong. So was Sun-jo.

PEAK EXPERIENCE

WE ARRIVED AT BASE CAMP just in time to see Josh get into a fistfight with someone. At 18,044 feet, though, it wasn't much of a fight.

An older, red-faced man took a swing, which Josh easily ducked and countered by pushing him in the chest. The man landed on his butt in the snow. After this it was pretty much over except for the shouting.

"I want a full refund!" the man shouted. "If you think I'm going to sit around Base Camp while you and the others climb to glory, you have another thing coming!" (He was obviously one of Josh's clients, and not a very happy one.)

It's hard to get up when you are out of breath, swaddled in down clothes, with crampons strapped to your boots. Josh offered his hand to help him up, but the man slapped it away.

"George, you're in no shape to go any farther up the mountain," Josh said. "You heard what Dr. Krieger said. You have a bad heart, which you should have told me about before you signed up."

"My heart's fine! That witch doctor of yours doesn't know what she's talking about."

A pretty woman stepped up next to Josh. "You have a heart murmur, George," she said with a slight German accent. "Blocked arteries would be my guess. You need to get it looked at as soon as you get off the mountain."

"Well, I'm getting off this stupid mountain today," George wheezed, getting to his feet. "And my first appointment is not going to be with my doctor. It's going to be with my attorney! I'll sue you for everything you have, Josh."

"If you want to sue me for saving your life," Josh said, "go ahead." He turned and started to walk away, then noticed us and stopped.

"Looks like you have an extra climbing permit," Zopa said.

"Two, actually. We had a woman leave two days ago, hacking up her larynx. Apparently I'm responsible because she's threatening to sue me, too."

Josh looked at me. The beard he had cut off for my arraignment was growing back in nicely. "So, how was it?" he asked.

"It was good."

He looked back at Zopa. "Can he make it up the mountain?"

Zopa shrugged.

Josh glanced over at the truck where Sun-jo, Yogi, and Yash were standing. "Do you have room to take George back down?"

Zopa nodded. "Those three are staying. That is if you have work."

"We'll see," Josh said without much enthusiasm. "We might need some Base Camp help, but with two less climbers we don't need any more climbing Sherpas."

He looked back at the small truck, then looked back at Zopa. "It'll be a tight fit. You'll have to haul George's wife down, too, and all their gear. She's in her tent sick as a dog. You'll need to get them both to the hospital as soon as you get to Kathmandu."

"There will be enough room," Zopa said. "I'm staying here, too. At least for a few days. I'll talk to the driver. He'll get them to Kathmandu safely."

Zopa started toward the truck but didn't get very far. A Jeep came roaring up and skidded to a stop, blocking his path.

Josh swore, then said under his breath, "Captain Shek. Be cool. Let me do the talking."

A tall Chinese officer in a crisp green uniform got out of the Jeep and walked up to us, frowning. "Papers!"

"Good afternoon," Josh said with a smile.

"No one go until I see papers!"

"Of course," Josh said.

But the captain was too late. Sun-jo, Yogi, and Yash were already gone. (Poof!)

"Show him your visa and passport," Josh said.

I dug them out of my pack and handed them over.

Captain Shek carefully scrutinized them, glancing between me and the photo.

"You climb?"

"He's my son," Josh answered. "He's on my climbing permit."

"Last name no match."

"He has his mother's name. We're divorced."

(I guess it was too complicated to explain that they were never married.)

The captain handed back my passport. Next he checked Zopa's papers, then the driver's. After he finished he locked his dark eyes on each of us and said, "We watching all you." He climbed back into the Jeep and drove away.

"He's not kidding about that," Josh said. "Captain Shek

and his men are always watching." He pointed to a small rise with a ramshackle building on top of it. "They have a spotting scope set up there, and the rumor is that he has night vision equipment as well. They monitor the radio transmissions, looking for violations. Shek's already booted two climbing parties this year. Try to stay clear of him."

"And he doesn't always show up dressed in uniform," Dr. Krieger warned. "He sometimes dresses like a climber and wanders around camp catching people unaware. I'll be in the Aid tent." She walked away.

"What do you think of Base Camp so far?" Josh asked.

Because of the argument and Captain Shek I hadn't paid much attention to the camp, but I saw now that it was gigantic. Red, blue, green, and yellow tents were scattered around for what seemed like a mile.

"How many people are here?"

"Three hundred fifty or so," Josh answered. "Maybe another fifty acclimatizing farther up the mountain."

Most of them must have been in their tents trying to stay warm because there weren't too many people wandering around. I looked at the temperature on my watch: fourteen degrees. According to the wind gauge (the watch Josh gave me did everything), the wind was blowing ten miles an hour, which brought the temperature down to three degrees above zero.

Josh looked me over. "You breathing okay? Any problems on the way up?"

Both were good questions considering this was only the second time I'd been this high on a mountain. The summer before I had almost made it to the top of Mount McKinley in Alaska. We were at 18,000 feet (2,000 feet short of the summit) when our guide turned us back because of weather.

"I've had a headache the past two days," I said. "But it's going away."

Josh pointed at George, who had returned to his tent and was angrily packing his gear. "My headache's going away, too," he said. "At least one of them."

He looked over at the truck. Sun-jo and the brothers had reappeared and were helping Zopa unload it. "Who's the kid?"

"His name's Sun-jo."

"Is he with Zopa?"

"Yeah."

"Interesting," he said. "Did Zopa tell you he was going to stay at Base Camp for a few days?"

I shook my head. "Like you said, Zopa doesn't talk much."

"Yeah . . . Well, he's up to something."

"Like what?"

Josh smiled. "He'll let us know when he's ready. Let's head over to Peak Experience headquarters. I'll introduce you to the Base Camp crew."

"Peak Experience?"

"I didn't name it after you exactly," Josh admitted. "But I probably should have."

"What are you talking about?"

"Peak Experience is my adventure travel company. We started it last year. Almost wish I hadn't now."

I followed him to a giant orange tent with PEAK EXPERIENCE tagged on the sides. The *A* in *Peak* looked like a mountain. He pulled back the flap and waved me through.

Inside were several people and more electronic equipment than I had ever seen in a tent at 18,000 feet (or any tent, for that matter): laptops, satellite phones, two-way radios, fax machines, television monitors, and other gizmos.

The crew was so busy talking on phones, listening to radios, tapping on keyboards, they didn't seem to notice us. None of them looked like climbers.

"What is all this?" I asked.

"This is what happens when you get old and start worrying about your future." He pointed to a pudgy guy talking on a satellite phone. "That guy over there is my business partner, Thaddeus Bowen. The rest of the people are support staff. There is another bunch of them back in the office in Chiang Mai, and some up on K2 and Annapurna."

"You're running three expeditions at the same time?"

He smiled. "Get this: Most of our clients are rank amateurs—some haven't been higher than twelve thousand feet. Stupid, huh? But I'm not alone. There are at least ten commercial operations like this at Base Camp. Some of them are running four separate expeditions. Things have changed since your mom and I were living out of the back of that rusty old van at El Cap."

When he said that he had clients I assumed he meant experienced climbers, nothing like this.

"People!" Josh said. "This is my son, Peak."

I felt a flush of pride. Some of them nodded, some smiled, though none of them fully stopped what they were doing. Thaddeus walked over, covering the mouthpiece of his satellite phone.

"How'd George take the news?"

"He took a punch at me," Josh said. "Says he's going to sue."

Thaddeus rolled his eyes. "Great. I'll call our attorney and tell him to get ready." He walked away resuming his phone conversation.

A woman came over and handed Josh a sheet of paper. "The film crew should be here later this afternoon. And I finally tracked down the whereabouts of Holly Angelo."

The name sounded familiar to me, but I couldn't remember where I'd heard it.

"Where is she?" Josh asked.

"She's with the film crew," the woman answered. "Apparently she came in on the same flight. The film crew is threatening to murder her. She brought along her own personal chef and massage therapist, and so much gear they had to rent a second truck."

"I told her she couldn't bring anybody," Josh said. "And to travel light."

"She didn't listen," the woman said. "She's also found out that you have an opening on your climbing permit. She wants to go to the top."

Josh swore. "How'd she find out about that?"

"Word travels fast at high altitudes."

"She's here to cover Peak, not herself."

"What do you mean?" I asked.

"I'll tell you about it later," Josh said distractedly. "Can you reach her on the sat phone?"

"If she's not in the middle of a massage," the woman answered, then started punching in numbers.

Josh turned to me. "I need to take care of this. There's a spot for your tent next to mine. The blue one out back. Why don't you go out and get set up."

Sun-jo helped me haul my gear and set up the tent. When we finished we took a little tour.

Now, you might be thinking that Base Camp on Everest would be one of the most pristine places on earth. The truth is that you have to watch where you step. And here's a tip: Avoid digging up yellow snow to melt for your drinking water. At ten degrees below zero no one strays far from his tent to take care of business. Everest Base Camp is a frozen outhouse/garbage dump with decades of crap, discarded food containers, and busted gear. I had read that some of the climbers and Sherpas were trying to clean it up, but by the looks of the camp they hadn't made much of a dent. Sardine cans, chip bags, cartons, toilet paper, and other trash blew around the tents like tumbleweed.

Climbers from all over the world were here. Japan, Bolivia, Mexico, Italy, Canada, Luxembourg . . . There were women's teams, military teams; there was even a team made up exclusively of people over fifty. (They had a placard outside their camp that read: THE GERIATRIC TEAM. BEWARE OF GRUMPY OLD CLIMBERS!)

You could pick out the commercial climbing operations by the size of their tents and their camp spots, which were usually the best on the slope. I counted eleven of them, and that's when it began to dawn on me that Josh might be just as cagey as old Zopa.

There was a lot of competition sitting on the mountain under those large tents. Getting a dozen clients to the summit could bring in as much as a million dollars, and if you were simultaneously mounting other expeditions on other 8,000-meter peaks, several million dollars.

If an Everest wannabe was going to plop down a hundred grand (or several thousand to get to one of the lower camps) who were they going to give their money to? The company with the best success rate? The company with the best safety record? Or maybe, the company who put the youngest person in the world on the world's tallest mountain, who also just happened to have the same first name as the company that put him on the top. And did you hear about him climbing those skyscrapers in New York?

Don't worry about the money. I'll get my portion back.

The film crew should be here later this afternoon.

She's here to cover Peak, not herself.

I suddenly remembered where I had seen the name Holly Angelo. It was a byline under an article about me climbing the skyscraper. She was the reporter who broke the news about who my real father was. Did she dig up this information on her own? Or did Josh give her a call and spill his guts?

The youngest person so far to reach the top of Everest was a fifteen-year-old Nepalese girl named Ming Kipa Sherpa.

If I were one year older I might still be in . . . I stopped in midstep.

"What's the matter?" Sun-jo asked.

"Nothing," I said.

Would Josh have bailed me out if I had already turned fifteen? I didn't think so. Was he using me? Probably. Did I mind? I wasn't sure at that point. He was paying more attention to me than he had my whole life.

"I'm going to head back," I said.

"I should go, too," Sun-jo said. "Zopa wants me to talk to the cook about helping in the mess tent."

"A job?" I asked.

"For room and board." Sun-jo smiled. "Or tent and food, I should say. Perhaps it will lead to something else."

Tent and food was not going to get the tuition paid. "I could talk to my father," I offered. "If I asked him, I think he'd hire you for more than tent and food."

Sun-jo shook his head. "We had better leave that up to Zopa. He brought me to the mountain. It is for him to decide."

ROCK WEASELS

RATHER THAN CONFRONT JOSH, I crawled into my tent, wrapped myself in my sleeping bag, and fell asleep.

I know what you're thinking: CHICKEN! Maybe you're right. But what was I going to say? "I will not be used, Father!" Or how about this: "Send me back to New York so I can do my time. Take that, Dad!"

Besides, I needed some sleep before I talked to him. Walking around at 18,000 feet wears you down. And it turned out that I didn't have to find him because he found me.

"You awake?" he asked.

"Yeah," I said, although I hadn't been until he stuck his head into my tent.

He crawled in and zipped the flap closed. "Did you get a chance to look around the camp?"

"A little. There's a lot of competition for your company up here."

"You noticed, huh? Next year there won't be so many commercial operations. There's only a finite number of people who have the money, time, and desire to get up this mountain. This will be the last year for a lot of the operations."

"Including Peak Experience?" I asked.

He grinned. "Your mom told me that you're smart," he said. "I guess you got that from her."

Flattery has never worked on me. "So, how much trouble are you in?"

"Like the judge said, I look good on paper. But the truth is, I'm in debt up to my crevasse."

Humor, on the other hand, always worked on me. I laughed.

"If we have a good season this year," he continued, "we might be able to recoup some of our losses next year. It's all riding on how many people we get to the summit in the next few weeks and how much publicity we get."

"Which is why I'm here," I said.

He gave me a sheepish look. "Not entirely," he said. "But yeah, that's one of the reasons."

That's the main reason, I thought. Might as well get it over with. "If I had been fifteen would you have come to New York?"

He hesitated, then said, "Probably not. I was right in the middle of leading a group of amateur climbers to Everest."

I would have liked it a lot better if he had come to New York to save me because *I* was in trouble, not because *he* was in trouble.

"The youngest Americans to top Everest are a couple of twenty-year-olds," he explained. "So, your being fifteen might have worked, but truthfully, getting a fourteen-year-old up there has a lot more sex appeal, especially after your climb in New York.

"There are a lot of celebrities climbing this year: a couple of rockers, an actor, a football player. There are seven documentary and TV crews on this side of the mountain alone, and just as many, if not more, on the south side. So, when we tried to get the media interested in our climb there were no takers. Without publicity we're circling the drain.

"Your skyscraper stunt was beamed all over the world. I knew about it before your mom called and asked if I could help out. Someone in our Chiang Mai office saw it on TV, figured out the connection, and called up here suggesting we try to put you on top. At first I told them no way, but then your mom called. I thought I could take care of your problem and mine at the same time."

"Did you talk to Mom about what we're doing?"

"Yeah, before I left Kathmandu."

"What did you tell her?"

"I told her I was going to take you on a climb, but I didn't tell her where."

"She's not going to like it when she finds out."

"Don't be so sure. She may not climb anymore, but she understands what it's all about. That's why she let you go to those climbing camps. She knows that I might risk my own life to summit, but I would never risk anyone else's, especially my own son's, to get to the top of a mountain."

"What's going to make her mad is your not telling her beforehand," I said.

"You're probably right, but the reason I didn't tell her is that we can't let this out until you're back down."

"What about the film crew?"

"They're not going to say anything. We're paying them. They work for us."

"What about Holly Angelo?"

He gave a deep, foggy sigh. (It was cold in the tent.)

"Blackmail," he said. "Or what amounts to it, anyway.

Somehow she figured it all out. I think she might have a line to Dr. Woo.

"And by the way, if you had flunked the physical I wouldn't have brought you up here. Period. I would have sent you on to Chiang Mai. And I did enroll you in the International School there.

"Anyway, Holly called me here last week and said that she was going to print a story about your Everest attempt unless I gave her an exclusive."

"And now she wants to climb the mountain herself," I said.

"Yeah, and it looks like I'm going to have to give her a shot. Otherwise, she's going to start filing reports as soon as she gets up here."

"Why do we have to keep it quiet?"

"Because of the Chinese," he said. "There's no age limit on this side of the mountain, but if they find out we're trying to put a fourteen-year-old on the top, they might pull our climbing permit. They've been trying to get a teenager to the summit for years. They wouldn't be too happy if an American teenager topped it before one of their own."

He let out a harsh laugh. "Politics, publicity, advertising, sponsorships, endorsements: Climbing has really gone downhill. I can't tell you how much I miss our rock rat days when we showed up at the base of a wall with a bag of trail mix, a bottle of water, and an old rope. We're rock weasels now, and it will never be the same."

"Josh!" A high-pitched scream pierced the cold mountain air.

"That would be Holly," Josh said.

"You know her voice?"

"I haven't heard it in fifteen years, but I'd recognize it anywhere. Kind of like fingernails scraping on a chalkboard."

"Josh!"

We both winced.

"Holly was on the circuit writing freelance articles when your mom and I were climbing. She actually wrote a couple of good pieces about us. She climbed, too—kind of." He shook his head. "It was a scary thing to watch."

"Josh!"

"So, I'll take you to the top," Josh said. "But only if I can do it without killing you. If you make it you'll be famous . . . and you'll help your old man live in comfort for the rest of his life. My plan is to sell the business in a few years and retire on the proceeds. Are we square?"

I wasn't sure about the famous part, and I wasn't happy about his reason for bringing me to Everest, but I did want to get to the top.

"We're square," I said. "But no more caginess. I want to know what's going on."

"It's a deal." He stuck out his gloved hand and we shook.

"Josh!"

He unzipped the flap and peeked out. "We'd better go and say hello before she causes an avalanche."

GASP

HOLLY ANGELO LOOKED like a redheaded scarecrow dressed in pink goose down.

She was over six feet tall with limbs like a daddy longlegs. As soon as she saw Josh she wrapped her arms around him with a shriek so loud every head for a quarter mile popped out of its tent like turtles coming out of their shells.

Standing next to her were several curious Sherpas, three camera guys, a personal chef, and a massage therapist. The chef and the massage therapist were shivering and would be dead before morning unless somebody found them warmer gear.

Josh wriggled out of her tentacles and held her at arm's length so she couldn't snag him again. "You haven't changed a bit," he said with his trademark grin. (Meaning, I think: "Holly, you are still a pain in the crevasse.")

Her hawklike brown eyes darted around for her next victim, which happened to be me. "Peeeeak!"

Luckily the drawn-out version of my name doubled her over with a coughing fit and she wasn't able to get to me. You would think that her chef or massage therapist would have come to her aid, but they just stood there shivering, watching their employer bent over clutching her knees.

"Bad cough," Josh said, when she was finally able to right herself.

"No big . . . *gasp* . . . deal. You know . . . *gasp* . . . the altitude and . . . *gasp* . . . dry air . . . *gasp* . . ."

"We'll have Doc Krieger take a look at you." He was still smiling but the grin looked a little more genuine. He did not want to take Holly Angelo up the mountain any farther than he had to. In her current condition it didn't look like she was going to get very far.

I followed him over to meet the film crew: JR, Will, and Jack. They all looked fit. He thanked them for coming up.

"Happy to be here," JR said, then whispered, "Do us a favor, Josh. Put us as far away from Holly as possible."

"No problem." Josh looked over at the gasping reporter.

Holly was already telling the Sherpas where to pitch her pink tent, which was only slightly smaller than the HQ tent.

Josh frowned when he saw she was erecting the monstrosity right next to his and my tent, but he didn't say anything to her. He looked back at JR and pointed to a spot about seventy-five feet away.

"Best I can do."

"Fine," JR said. He and the others headed over to the spot with their gear.

Josh rubbed his temples. "I probably don't need to tell you this, but you need to be very careful about what you say to Holly. She's a reporter and anything you tell her is fair game. Just remember that she is more interested in herself and her career than she is in you."

"What about the film crew?" I asked.

"No worries there. We own the footage. When we edit it down we'll make you look good no matter how you screw up." He grinned. "Just kidding. Let's go over to the mess tent and I'll introduce you to the other climbers. Just keep in mind, they know you're my son, but we haven't told them that we're trying to get you to the top."

"Why?"

"Because they've paid upward to a hundred grand to summit. In a way, we're using their money to get you up there. They might get upset."

"So, what am I supposed to tell them?"

"That you're here with me and don't expect to make it past Camp Four or Five." He looked back over in Holly's direction. "I guess I better fill her in, too, so she keeps her big mouth shut. I'll meet you over at the mess tent." He sighed, put on his charming grin again, and headed toward Holly, who was shrieking orders at the Sherpas. The Sherpas, for the most part, were ignoring her every command.

THE MESS TENT was nearly as big as the HQ tent, but a lot more crowded. It was also smoky from the kerosene lamps and stoves, and cigarettes. None of the clients were smoking, but almost every Sherpa had a cigarette dangling out of his mouth as he stood to the side holding a plate of food.

Sun-jo was manning the noodles. I went over to say hello.

"How's it going?"

"What was that terrible sound outside?" he asked.

"A reporter."

"Injured?"

"Not yet."

I looked around and noticed Zopa wasn't there. "Where's Zopa?"

Sun-jo shrugged.

A climber walked over and held out his plate. Sun-jo

scooped some noodles onto it with a big smile. The man sniffed the pile, grunted, then walked away.

"What do you think of your fellow climbers?" Sun-jo asked.

"I didn't like that guy," I said, then looked around the tent and did a head count. Seven women, sixteen men (including the rude grunter). Ten of them had signed up for a summit attempt. I tried to pick out which ones they were, but it was hard to figure out. Fitness helped, but getting through the death zone was more about your blood oxygenation, and luck: things even the fittest climber had absolutely no control over. Most of the climbers appeared to be in their thirties or early forties, and of these, only five or six looked in good enough shape to get to the top. I could see why Josh was worried about the climbing season.

I told Sun-jo that I was surprised to see the Sherpas smoking.

"Most of them believe they will die on the mountain," he said. "So, why not enjoy themselves while they wait?"

"But doesn't smoking mess up their climbing?"

"Only if they run out of tobacco," Sun-jo answered. "But Zopa brought up several cartons of cigarettes to sell to them."

Monks weren't supposed to use any stimulants. I guess this rule didn't preclude them from selling them.

"Don't look so surprised," Sun-jo said. "Zopa will give the profits to the Tibetan monks. They are very poor. As you saw on the way here, the Chinese are not favorable toward them."

"Cagey monk reason number two," I said.

"What?"

"Never mind," I said. "I guess I'd better mingle with the other climbers."

"Do you want some noodles? They are very good."

"Sure."

They were good.

I'm not much of a mingler, which drove Rolf crazy, since he is perhaps the greatest mingler on the planet. I have seen him go up to a complete stranger and ask for the time (even though Rolf always has a perfectly good watch on his wrist) just to get a conversation started. But I don't think even Rolf could have cracked this crowd.

They had been at Base Camp for a couple of weeks now and had bonded into inseparable groups. This wasn't the first time I'd run into this. GSS always got out late for summer. By the time I arrived at climbing camp the other kids had already picked their climbing partners. This left me with the kids who had virtually no previous climbing experience, or if I was lucky, the climbing instructor.

Vincent told me that good writers are lousy minglers. They are too busy eavesdropping, or as he puts it: *Gathering grist for their literary mills.*

So, because no one was paying an iota of attention to me, I just wandered around gathering grist. . . .

"WE SHOULD HAVE *been up at ABC by now."*

(ABC stands for Advance Base Camp, which is the next permanent camp up the north side of the mountain.)

"We would have been if Josh hadn't ditched us for his so-called son."

(The so-called son was standing five feet away from the two guys talking.)

"I didn't even know he had a son."

"Neither did I—and I read every article ever written about him before I plopped down my life savings."

"I hear the reason we're stuck down here is because he's waiting for a film crew and reporter from New York."

"They came in today. No film, no glory, I guess. Josh is a publicity hound."

"DR. LEAH KRIEGER *is the coldest fish I've ever met."*

"Straight from Nazi Germany, if you ask me. I think she's here to perform experiments on us, not treat us."

"Poor George. Do you think he really had a heart condition?"

"I don't know, but I heard that George's wife begged Krieger to put in a bad report. She never wanted him to climb the mountain in the first place, and she's the one with all the money. Before they got married, George didn't have two pennies to rub together."

"I WANDERED OVER *to William Blade's camp this morning. I couldn't tell if I saw him or not, but I think I got close because one of his bodyguards rushed over and blocked my way as I tried to walk past his tent."*

"Think he'll make it to the top?"

"He already has, as far as I'm concerned."

"You know what I mean: the summit."

"If he can't do it on his own two feet, his bodyguards are big enough to carry him up there on their backs."

(William Blade was a famous actor. I'd seen most of his films and thought he was great.)

"I heard there are three people up at ABC with HAPE. They're coming down tomorrow."

"Well, they're luckier than the guy who died on the south side

yesterday. Stepped out of his tent in the middle of the night to pee. Idiot was wearing slippers. He slid two hundred yards down a slope into a crevasse so deep the Sherpas say he's probably still falling."

"He should have been wearing crampons."

"Or at least carrying his ax so he could self-arrest."

(SELF-ARREST HAS NOTHING TO DO with law enforcement. It's one of the first things they teach you in mountaineering. If you start sliding down an icy slope with nothing to grab on to, you'd better know how to stop yourself by digging in your crampons, or punching your ax into the ice and hanging on for dear life. All steep slopes end badly, in trees, solid walls, or deep holes. "Screaming in terror doesn't slow you down one bit," one of my instructors told me. "If you want to live you'd better learn to avoid the void." Self-arrest wasn't my best climbing skill. Hearing about a guy dying because he stepped out to go to the bathroom made my skin crawl.)

"JOSH IS SO CUTE! *What do you think he'd do if I snuck into his tent one night?"*

"I don't think that's included in the permit fee."

"If you wait until you're above twenty thousand feet nothing will happen. More than your lungs shut down at—"

THE MOST INTERESTING PART of my grist gathering got cut off by the entrance of Holly Angelo.

"Hello everyone! . . . *gasp* . . . My name is Holly Angelo. I'm a journalist from New York and I'll be joining you . . . *gasp* . . . on top of the world!"

Holly did not mingle, she mangled. Her gasps were met with other gasps, but not because of the thin air, although a lot of the oxygen was sucked out of the mess tent when she walked in.

All conversation stopped.

A plate of food dropped.

A Sherpa nearly swallowed the cigarette he was smoking, then made a mad dash for the back entrance with five or six other Sherpas. I was going to join them, but I was too slow. Talons with bright red fingernail polish latched onto my parka.

"Where . . . *gasp* . . . do you think . . . *gasp* . . . you're going?"

Holly whipped me around to face her with surprising strength.

"Uh . . . ," I stammered.

"I need to talk to you."

"Uh . . . okay."

"Now . . . *gasp* . . . I have seen your pitiful . . . *gasp* . . . tent and I think you will be a lot . . . *gasp* . . . more comfortable . . . *gasp, gasp* . . . in my tent."

I thought I would faint.

"I have a lot . . . *gasp* . . . of room . . . *gasp* . . . an extra cot . . ."

No one hauled a cot all the way up to Base Camp, but she had a spare.

". . . and my food is much better than . . . *gasp* . . . this swill. Pierre is creating something right now . . . *gasp* . . . and Ralph has his massage table set up if you need a rubdown."

"Uh . . ."

"Your father said it was up to . . . *gasp* . . . you."

Thanks, Dad.

Coughing fit . . .

I thought about sneaking out while she was coughing.

She would straighten up and ole Peak would just be gone. Poof! Then I thought about what Josh had told me: *Be very careful about what you say*... and figured that it also applied to what I did. It's rude to disappear when someone is hacking their lungs out.

"We have so much to discuss," she said when the fit was over, which seemed to have helped her gasping. "Your mom and I go way back. We've been friends for years."

If that had been the case I would have recognized her name the first time I saw it in the byline above the article she'd written.

"She would never forgive me if I didn't watch out for you up here."

"I appreciate the offer," I said, trying to give her my version of Josh's charming grin (which probably looked more like a scowl), "but I think I'll stay in my own tent."

This was returned with a genuine scowl. I didn't care. There was no way I was going to become her tent mate.

"But you will have your meals with me," she said, as if this wasn't even open to question.

I was holding the plate of noodles, which had cooled and congealed and wasn't looking its best at that moment.

"Not every meal," I hedged. "But yeah, I'll eat with you once in a while."

Her scowl deepened and I think she was about to say something nasty, but I was saved by Josh coming into the tent.

"Okay, people," he announced. "Tomorrow we head up to ABC."

A cheer went up.

"It'll take us three days and two nights to get up there if

everything goes well. We'll spend two nights at ABC, then come back down. You know the routine."

"Climb high, sleep low," the team chanted in unison.

"Leah will check you tonight to get a baseline on your blood, et cetera, then check you again up at ABC to see how you're doing."

This news was met with much less enthusiasm.

"She's waiting for you in the Aid tent." He pinned a sheet of paper on the tent pole. "She wrote down your exam times. Don't be late."

"Heil Hitler," a climber muttered under his breath.

Josh shot him a look and he turned bright red. Nobody got up to the summit unless the expedition leader said they were going up. It was best to stay on the captain's good side.

"What about the *puja* ceremony?" someone asked.

A *puja* is a Buddhist blessing ritual that most climbing parties went through prior to going up the mountain.

"We'll be going up to ABC two more times in the next few weeks," Josh said. "We'll hold our *puja* before one of those. I want to get an early start tomorrow."

A couple of the Sherpas didn't look too happy about skipping the *puja.*

"Pack just enough food for the trip," Josh continued. "It will be a hard climb and you don't want to be carrying any more weight than necessary."

The speech ended and the climbers gathered around the sheet. Josh walked over to Holly and me.

"You two won't be coming," he said. "I'm holding JR, Jack, and Will back, too. You haven't acclimatized enough to go higher."

"Then why don't you wait a few days?" Holly asked. "We can . . . *gasp* . . . all go up together."

It was a good question. Mostly because I couldn't imagine being stuck in camp alone with Holly for the next several days.

Josh lowered his voice. "I'd like nothing better than to wait, but most of these people have been here for weeks. If I don't get them higher they'll riot. A third of them have only signed up for ABC. When we come back down they're gone, which will make things a lot easier around here. I'll take you up to ABC as soon as I get back down. I can't hold them back because of latecomers."

LATECOMERS

JOSH'S ABSENCE WASN'T AS BAD as I thought, although Zopa worked Sun-jo and me like dogs.

The morning Josh headed up the mountain he had us build a six-foot-tall cairn out of rocks around a central flagpole for the *puja* blessing ceremony. We then placed smaller poles in the ground around the main pole and strung up dozens of prayer flags between them on strings. The flags come in five colors—red, green, yellow, blue, and white—representing the earth's five elements: fire, wood, earth, water, and iron. As the flags flutter in the wind they release the prayers written on them and pacify the gods.

When we finished Josh had Sun-jo and me gather gear from our team's tents and lean it against the cairn to be blessed.

Zopa held the ceremony that evening for a German and Italian climbing party going up the next morning, and for our group in absentia, which he said wasn't ideal, but it sometimes worked. He recited several Buddhist prayers, then asked the mountain for permission for us to climb it—in German, English, and Italian, which was impressive.

The ceremony took about three hours, and just as it was ending, a black bird landed on the main flagpole, which Zopa said was very auspicious.

"What kind of bird was that?" I asked as we headed back to camp. It looked kind of like a crow or a raven.

Sun-jo shrugged.

IT TURNED OUT that even though Holly Angelo was right next door to me, she was relatively easy to avoid.

She never left her tent before ten. I was out of mine by seven every morning. Because there were so many people in the camp, it was easy to get lost among the tents, unless you were Holly, who wore the most garish-colored snowsuits on the slope. I could pick her out a mile away and hide.

She did manage to snag me for dinner the fourth night Josh was gone. I made the mistake of heading back to my tent to drop off my ice ax before dinner (Zopa had been giving Sun-jo and me self-arrest lessons), and Holly was waiting for me like a guard dog.

The food was better than what they offered in the mess tent, but the atmosphere was grim. Ralph sat on his massage table with a permanent pout on his face, as if he were waiting for customers he knew would never come.

Chef Pierre watched every bite of food I took and muttered about the barbaric cooking conditions at 18,000 feet.

And Holly . . . Well, my headache came back, but it wasn't from the altitude. Inside a tent her voice was shrill enough to sour yak butter. She was no longer gasping, which I missed because the pauses gave my ears a chance to rest.

I thought she was going to interview me, but it turned out that I was there to listen to her interview herself. During the two-hour nonstop monologue she filled me in on her life, year by boring year. I didn't really start tuning in until she turned eighteen, but even then it wasn't very interesting.

She'd been married three times and her current husband lived in Rome and she rarely saw him. She came from a wealthy family and didn't have to work for a living. She became a "journalist" (as she called it) against her father's wishes because she felt it was her "moral responsibility to tell the truth." (I didn't mention that in the article she'd written about us there were several things that were blatantly untrue.) I also think she exaggerated her climbing conquests, because when I asked her what mountains she had climbed, she said, "You know, all the big ones," and quickly changed the subject to dreams, asking if I ever have them.

"Yes."

"Well, let me tell you about one I had just last night," she said.

I hate hearing about people's dreams, but I was spared by the arrival of William Blade and three bodyguards the size of yetis.

In his films William Blade had been shot, stabbed, starved, beaten, and tortured, but he had never looked worse than when he hobbled into Holly's tent.

"His back went out," one of the bodyguards explained. "We were wondering if your massage therapist can put him right."

"Of course!" Holly said, pushing things out of the way (including me) to make room.

Ralph smiled for the first time since he had arrived on the mountain and gleefully began laying out liniments and lotions and flexing his muscles (which weren't very impressive).

I stayed long enough to watch them get Blade out of his clothes and onto the table, where he started yelling and swearing at everyone in the tent as if we were personally responsible for his bad back.

I didn't see what happened the next day (Zopa had Sun-jo and me climbing a treacherous icefall outside camp) but we heard all about it when we got back that afternoon.

After Ralph worked his magic on the film hero's back, Blade offered to pay him twice as much as Holly was paying to move over to his camp. Apparently, Ralph couldn't get his gear together fast enough. When Pierre saw this he begged Blade to take him, too, which he did, leaving Holly absolutely alone in her giant pink tent screaming in rage.

The bet was she was going to quit the mountain. The only person who put cash down on her staying was Zopa. He met everyone's wager with the money he had gotten from his cigarette sales.

It was hours after the incident before Holly emerged from her tent. It turned out that she wasn't about to head home to her Upper East Side penthouse apartment.

We were in the mess tent waiting to hear from Josh and the team up at ABC. They were supposed to leave that morning for Base Camp, but got pinned down by a snowstorm. We had heard that some of the people up there had HAPE, but the storm had knocked out further radio communication, so we didn't know who was sick or how bad it was. If the team wasn't able to start down the next day, the situation would turn critical. They had brought only enough food for two days at ABC.

A couple of the Sherpas were talking about hauling up some food for them.

"Not tonight," Zopa said. "The storm is moving down the mountain."

The Sherpas and a small group of other climbers were arguing with Zopa about his weather prediction when Holly sauntered into the mess tent.

"I'm going to the top," she announced calmly, then walked over and got a plate of food.

The only person smiling was Zopa. And why not? He had just won a pot of money—literally. The mess cook had been keeping the bets in a ten-gallon rice cooker, which was now overflowing with rupees.

Sun-jo had told me that if Zopa won the bet he would give the money to the Tibetan monks.

They would have to wait to get their cash. I didn't know this yet, but just like Holly, Zopa had no plans to go home anytime soon.

"The snow is here," one of the Sherpas said.

"That's impossible," I said. I hadn't been in the tent more than twenty minutes. When I'd walked over from HQ there wasn't a cloud in the sky.

The cook pulled the flap back and we stared outside in disbelief. The snow was so thick I wasn't sure how I was going to find my tent.

GAMOW BAG

I MADE IT AS FAR as the HQ tent, but no farther that night. The storm dumped about four feet of snow on Base Camp. It was much worse up at ABC.

Josh managed to get through on the radio only once during the night. It was scratchy and broken-up, but we think he said there were sustained winds of seventy-three miles an hour and gusts of over a hundred. The team members were hunkered down in their tents, but there was no way for Josh to check on them because of the weather.

At first light he dug out and reported in again. "Base, we're all accounted for, but we have two cases of HAPE. Francis and Bill. One severe, one mild. How's the weather down there?"

"Clear," the radio operator, Sparky, answered. "I just checked the meteorological maps and there's nothing new coming in until tonight."

"When?"

"Storm's ETA is nineteen hundred, give or take several hours."

Josh gave a harsh laugh, followed by a coughing fit. When he finally recovered he said, "I hear you on that weather window. I'll start everyone down as soon as we get them rehydrated. We're giving Bill extra Os and he's responding well. I think he'll be able to make it down on his own. Leah and I will follow behind him with Francis and a couple Sherpas. We'll give Bill a hand if he needs it. We're trying to get Francis into a Gamow Bag."

Francis was the guy who grunted at the noodles. A Gamow bag (pronounced "GAM-off") was invented by Igor Gamow in the late 1980s and has saved a lot of climbers from dying of HAPE. It's like an airtight body bag. At high altitudes the air pressure is extremely low. You zip the victim inside a Gamow bag, pump it full of air until it's about the same pressure as it would be at sea level, and bingo, the climber can breathe again . . . hopefully.

"We'll start looking for the first climbers in about eight hours, then," Sparky said. "Be careful coming down. Avalanche risk is high."

"Keep us posted on the weather."

"Roger."

I DUG MY TENT OUT of the snow, then Zopa asked Sun-jo and me to dig out Holly's tent, which took us hours. She didn't help us, but she did keep us supplied with hot tea and cookies.

Late that afternoon the first of our team members started to straggle in, looking like zombies from *Night of the Living Dead.* It took them each three mugs of steaming sweet tea in the mess tent before they were finally able to put a coherent sentence together.

"It was a nightmare. . . . The snow started a thousand feet below ABC. It was so thick we had to fix a rope and tie ourselves together so we didn't lose anyone."

"Couldn't see a bloody thing past your eyelashes. Then it *really* started snowing."

"Twenty-two below at ABC without the windchill. We nearly froze to death trying to get our tents up."

The guy talking gingerly pulled the glove off his right hand. Three fingers were discolored and blistered. "Krieger says I'll keep the digits, but the little toe on my left foot is going to slough off in about a week. Never liked that toe, anyway." He laughed, but it wasn't a merry sound. "I'd show it to you, but it would just make you sick."

"The blizzard wasn't the worst of it," another climber said. "Not by a far sight." He was a cowboy from Abilene, Texas. "An avalanche hit us at about two in the morning. Sounded like the biggest dang stampede you ever heard. Wiped out seven tents. Didn't lose a soul, thank the Lord, but we had to double and triple up in the remaining tents like sardines."

"Then the food ran out," the man with the frostbitten fingers said. "Josh only had us bring enough for the trip up and back. This morning there wasn't a raisin to eat between us. We're lucky it cleared up. A couple more days and we would have starved to death."

"You're right about that, partner," the Texan agreed. "When I crawled out this morning I was eyeing one of them yaks with murder in my heart. Guess we should have had that dang *puja* ceremony before we started up the hill."

"Where's my—where's Josh?" I asked.

"Him and Krieger are still haulin' Francis down," the Texan drawled. "They didn't leave till late, from what I hear. Turns out Francis is claustrophobic. Should have guessed it. He's always sleeping with half his head outside the tent door. He about went plumb crazy when they zipped him into that bag. The only thing that saved him was that he passed out after a bit."

You might be thinking that the above conversation was a little coldhearted. And you'd be right. It was ten below zero outside, slightly warmer in the mess tent but not by much. When you are exhausted, having a hard time catching your breath, freezing, starving, waiting for your little toe to drop off, you have other things on your mind than the welfare of your fellow climbers.

Zopa waved Sun-jo and me over to him and told us to get our gear. We were going up the mountain to help Josh and Leah.

JR, WILL, AND JACK joined us. They had been filming our climbing lessons with Zopa the past few days, and I wasn't sure they were coming with us to help or to get footage of the Gamow bag in action.

I didn't think a thousand feet would make that much of a difference, but at that altitude even a hundred feet made a difference. Having to plow through freshly fallen snow didn't help. About every twenty steps I stopped, sucking in ragged breaths of freezing air. At this stage, my hope of getting to the summit, a mile and a half above where I was currently suffocating, seemed about as likely as me flying a Gamow bag to Jupiter. My only consolation was that Sun-jo and the film crew were having as much trouble as I was.

The one person who wasn't affected was Zopa. He'd wait for us until we were about fifty yards behind him, then continue up the Rongbuk Glacier like a mountain goat breaking trail.

By late afternoon there was still no sign of Josh and the others. If we didn't find them soon, we'd be searching in the dark, but even worse, clouds were starting to come in.

Zopa let us catch up to him just as the sun started slipping behind the mountain.

"Maybe they're spending the night at Camp Two or the intermediate camp," JR suggested between gasps.

There are two camps on the way up to ABC: an intermediate camp, and Camp Two, which lies three-quarters of the way up to ABC. The intermediate camp was nowhere in sight, which meant we weren't nearly as far up the mountain as it felt.

"And if they are not at the intermediate camp or Camp Two?" Zopa asked. (Meaning if Josh and Dr. Krieger had passed the camps, or hadn't reached them yet, they could freeze to death.)

"Good point," JR conceded. "What should we do?"

Zopa looked down the glacier, then squinted up at the darkening sky.

"A storm is coming," he said. "You can get down to Base Camp in an hour and a half, maybe two hours. If you leave now you can beat it."

JR gave him a skeptical look. We had been climbing for over four hours now.

"Downhill," Zopa said by way of explanation. "The trail is broken. Don't wander off it."

"What about you?" I asked.

He pulled his headlamp out of his pack and strapped it around his parka hood, then started to slip his pack back on. "I know your father. He will not watch that man die. He will try to get him off the mountain."

I think all of us wanted to go back down to Base Camp (I know I did), but none of us wanted to go down without Zopa, especially with bad weather moving in.

We put on our headlamps and followed Zopa's light.

Two hours later, in the dark, with the snow beginning to fall, we spotted two headlamps flickering a few hundred yards above us.

Josh and Leah looked completely done in. I don't think they would have made it much farther on their own. And I don't know who was happier to see who. They were happy we were there to help get Francis down, and we were happy to find them because it meant we got to go down.

"Did you bring Os?" Josh asked, kind of slurring his words.

Zopa pulled an oxygen tank and mask out of his pack. Josh cranked up the regulator and handed it to Leah, who took in several deep lungfuls. Josh was next. When he finished he offered it to us, but we all bravely shook our heads. We hadn't been up as long or as high as he and Leah, and the only reason they took hits was because they were exhausted. Climbers usually didn't start sucking Os until they got to Camp Five.

Zopa pointed to the bag. "How is he?"

"Alive . . . at least the last time we looked. But he has HAPE bad."

JR pointed his headlamp at the transparent window on the top of the bag, but it was too fogged up to see inside.

"You still with us, Francis?" Josh shouted.

I thought I heard a muffled reply, but it was hard to tell in the howling wind.

"He's writing a message," Leah said.

We stared as a feeble, backward sey appeared in the condensation on the window.

Josh managed to laugh, then looked at Leah. "Should we let him out?"

She shook her head.

"You're the doctor." He squatted and got closer to the bag. "Help has arrived, Francis! We'll have you down to Base Camp soon!"

Soon turned out to be four more hours. The glacier was steep and icy. We had to place ice screws and lower the bag on ropes a few feet at a time so it didn't take off like a toboggan.

We stumbled into Base Camp long after midnight. The camp was usually lit up like a Christmas tree with blue, red, and green tent lights, but this late, most of the climbers were asleep. We hauled the Gamow into the Aid tent and laid it on a cot. Leah pulled off her outer and inner thermal gloves with her teeth, then slowly unzipped the bag.

"How are you feeling?" she asked.

Francis was the color of a corpse. He blinked his eyes open and managed to give her a weak smile. He whispered, "I'm not claustrophobic anymore."

Leah smiled and put a stethoscope to his chest. "But you still have HAPE."

"I'm not going to the summit?"

"Not this year," Josh said, looking just as disappointed as Francis. He had another opening on his climbing permit.

WE LEFT FRANCIS AND LEAH and went into the mess tent. A handful of the team, staff, and Sherpas were still up drinking tea and playing cards. Josh reported on Francis's condition. When he finished he asked how Bill was.

"Not too good," the Texan answered. "He doesn't want to go back up."

Josh swore. Another climber down—and no one had climbed higher than ABC yet.

The mess tent cleared out pretty fast after that, leaving me, Sun-jo, Zopa, and Sparky. It felt good to drink hot tea and to breathe and have air actually fill my lungs. I felt like I was sitting in an oxygen tent, not a mess tent.

"Peak and Miss Angelo need to get up to ABC," Zopa said.

"I know," Josh said. "I was going to take them and the film crew up when I got back, but I'll have to wait a few days now. I'm wiped."

"I'll take them all up tomorrow," Zopa offered.

I couldn't even imagine walking back up the glacier in a few hours, but I couldn't protest in front of Josh or Zopa. I wished that JR, Will, and Jack hadn't headed to their tents after filming Francis being freed from the Gamow bag. If they had been there to hear Zopa's suggestion, I'm sure they would have protested for me.

"I can't ask you to do that," Josh said.

"You didn't ask me," Zopa said. "I offered. They need to go up. The weather will break in a few hours."

"Not according to the satellite maps I just looked at," Sparky said.

Zopa shrugged. "The maps are wrong."

"What about Holly?" Josh asked.

"I had a doctor from another camp look at her earlier today," Zopa answered. "She can go."

Josh grinned. "So, you already had this figured out before you came up to get me."

Zopa ignored the comment. "We will take some of the porters and yaks," he said. "Resupply what was lost in the storm. There are some Sherpas I would like to visit at ABC before I leave the mountain."

"Did you talk to Pa-sang?"

Pa-sang was Josh's sirdar, who I had seen around camp but had never officially met. He was constantly rushing around, yelling at the porters, arguing with Sherpas, or in the HQ tent talking to the Base Camp crew.

"He had the porters pack what was needed this afternoon," Zopa answered.

Josh looked at me. "Are you ready for twenty-one thousand feet?"

I said I was, but I had some serious doubts. I hoped Zopa was wrong about the weather.

ABC

THE NEXT MORNING I poked my head through the tent flap.

Crystal clear, twenty-eight degrees, no wind—by far the best weather we'd had since getting to Base Camp—and I could not have been more disappointed.

I had a sore throat and it felt like the muscles and joints inside my skin had been replaced with broken glass.

Sun-jo was sitting outside waiting for me, dressed in my former clothes, including my so-called junk boots. And there was an added touch: The Peak Experience logo had been sewn on both the parka and his stocking cap. I thought Zopa had traded all that stuff away. Why was Sun-jo wearing my clothes?

"You do not look well," he said.

"I do not feel well," I croaked back at him. "What's with the clothes?"

"They didn't fit you," he answered. "Zopa gave them to me."

I was too out of it to pursue it any further. I reached back into the tent for my water bottle and found it was frozen solid. I was so tired the night before, I had forgotten to put it in the sleeping bag with me to keep it from freezing. I'd spent hours packing and repacking my gear for the trip up to ABC.

Sun-jo pulled his water bottle out of his backpack. I took

a deep swig and handed it back, wondering why he had a backpack.

"Are you going up to ABC with us?"

"Yes," he answered. "And I would like to leave before the herders. I don't like stepping in yak dung."

"Me either," I said, although I had never seen yak dung. The porters kept yaks corralled at the far end of camp. I hadn't been over there yet, but you could sure smell the shaggy bovines when the wind blew from that direction.

I wondered why Zopa hadn't mentioned Sun-jo going up to ABC with us the night before, but I was too tired, hungry, and worried about the climb to ask Sun-jo about it right then. "Guess we'd better try to wake up Holly."

"She and Zopa have already left," Sun-jo said.

I looked at my watch in a panic, but it was only nine o'clock. "When did they leave?"

"Two hours ago."

"Why didn't Zopa wake me up?" I asked (although I was glad for the extra sleep).

"Miss Holly is a slow climber. We will overtake them."

I grabbed my gear and checked it one last time, then we went over to the mess tent to get something to eat. The only person inside was the cook. I was disappointed Josh wasn't there to see me off, but considering what he had been through the past few days, I couldn't blame him for sleeping in.

Halfway through my breakfast, JR, Will, and Jack dragged in, blurry-eyed and irritable, but after half an hour of coffee and carbs they began to perk up.

"Let's get this over with," Will said, smearing glacial cream on his face to prevent it from burning.

AT FIRST IT APPEARED that Holly was a faster climber than Sun-jo thought, but her speed was explained a few hours later when we finally caught up to her near a stream of glacial meltwater: Zopa had been carrying both his and Holly's heavy backpack as they made their way up the steep glacier.

Even without the backpack she was having a hard time catching her breath. She tried to smile when she saw us but couldn't quite manage it. Zopa looked a little haggard, too, which wasn't too surprising considering he was carrying as much weight as a yak.

Speaking of which, the yak herd had been gaining on us all day long and were now less than a hundred yards behind. Each yak carried over a hundred pounds of supplies *and* their own fodder—there was nothing else for them to eat this high.

With a grim expression Zopa looked at the long line of animals. I guess he didn't want to trudge through their dung anymore than we did.

"Those cows are going to ruin our shots," JR said.

"They're not cows, they're yaks," I said. "And how are they going to ruin your shots?"

"We're filming you, not a bunch of herders and their yaks."

I thought that at 19,000 feet all my hot buttons were out of reach, but JR had just managed to punch one of them dead center. I hated television documentaries where they filmed the intrepid scientist, climber, or explorer in the middle of some dreadfully hostile environment *all alone.* Oh yeah? Then who's operating the camera as they battle the elements *all alone*?

Back at Base Camp I had overheard climbers complaining about the "filthy" porters and herders and their "stinking" yaks. When something was missing from one of the camps, the porters and herders were always the first suspects.

Sure, I didn't want to step in yak dung, but it was pretty humbling to hear those same herders and porters in their cheap boots, ratty clothes, and heavy packs coming up behind us with the strength and breath to whistle, chant, and sing as they hauled *our* gear up the mountain. None of us were whistling or singing and we were carrying a tenth of what they had on their backs.

"Without those herders, yaks, and porters we wouldn't be here," I said to JR. "Leaving them out of the film is like leaving Everest out of the film. They're more important to a climber getting to the summit than the climber."

I didn't have enough breath for any more, but I think I made my point because Zopa laughed, long and hard (which is hard to do at that altitude). And when the yaks and herders and porters reached us JR filmed the entire procession crossing the stream, including the bloody spots in the snow left by the yaks that had cut their hooves on sharp rocks.

We gladly followed their dung trail all the way up to the intermediate camp. The camp wasn't exactly what I expected.

It was located at the very edge of an unstable cliff above a roaring glacial river. Behind us was a slope that looked like it was going to come tumbling down on top of us. I pointed out these two potential disasters to Zopa, and as an exclamation mark, a boulder popped loose and came tumbling down the slope, sliding to a stop about fifty feet from where we were standing.

"It's level," Zopa said as if a comfortable sleep were all that mattered before we were crushed to death.

I looked around at the others. None of them seemed bothered, but that might have been because they were so exhausted they could barely move. I knew exactly how they felt. The simplest tasks seemed to take forever and we weren't even up at ABC yet. There were three higher camps above that.

After setting up our tent (Sun-jo and I had decided to bunk together so we didn't have to carry up an extra tent) we set up Holly's. She hadn't uttered a single word since we'd caught up to her. She was sitting slumped on a flat rock like a puppet with its strings cut, watching us through dull, lifeless eyes.

Sun-jo went to help Zopa and the other Sherpas get dinner ready, and I walked over and asked Holly how she was doing.

She took several deep breaths, and on the last exhale managed a wheezy "Fine."

At sea level anyone who looked like she did would be in the back of an ambulance on their way to emergency, but at 19,028 feet the emergency threshold was proportionately higher. Even so, I didn't like Holly's chances for getting any farther up the mountain in the condition she was in.

A shot of Os would perk her right up, but it would also defeat the purpose of acclimatization. Her body was actually climbing as she was slumped on that cold rock, which was the whole purpose of climb high, sleep low. . . .

"Red blood cells are multiplying by the millions to protect our bodies from the thin air. These new red cells stick around during the rest periods at lower altitudes, making it easier the next time you go up. So even though—"

"Shut up, Peak," Holly managed to say with a small smile.

"What?"

"I know . . . *gasp* . . . how . . . *gasp* . . . red blood cells . . . *gasp* . . . work."

I stared at her completely dumbfounded until I realized that somewhere in the middle of my thoughts I had started talking out loud without realizing it, which should give you some idea of what kind of shape *I* was in.

"Sorry."

Holly nodded. "Help me to my tent."

When I got her up she swayed, but a couple of shallow breaths steadied her. It took us a good five minutes to walk the fifteen feet to the tent, and by the time we got there we were both gasping. It felt like somebody had cut *my* strings. What was happening to me?

I deposited Holly in her tent, then slowly made my way over to Sun-jo and Zopa, wondering if I was going to make it there without collapsing. Zopa handed me a cup. I took it from him, but I wasn't sure what I was supposed to do with it.

"Drink," he said.

Oh yeah, I thought sluggishly. *A cup. You drink from it.*

That first sip flowed down my esophagus and hit my belly like some kind of magic elixir. "What is this stuff?"

Zopa stared at me. "Tea," he said. "With sugar."

"What kind of tea?"

"Plain old green tea."

He reached into the inside pocket of my Gortex coat, pulled out my water bottle, and shook it. It was nearly full.

"Dehydration," he said. "You are not drinking enough. This will kill you faster than the thin air." He nodded toward Sun-jo, who also had his hands wrapped around a mug of tea. "Sun-jo is guilty, too."

I hadn't felt thirsty all day, but I knew Zopa was right. If you waited to drink until you were thirsty at this altitude it might be too late.

"Holly!" I said with alarm, thinking she was suffering from dehydration, too.

Zopa shook his head. "Miss Holly has had plenty of fluids," he said. "I made certain."

"She's not doing well," I said.

"I have seen worse," Zopa said. "And some of those made it to the summit. You can never tell who the mountain will allow and who it will not."

I HAD A MISERABLE NIGHT.

I went a little overboard in my hydration and had to get up three times to pee. Then, it seemed that every time I started to doze off, a boulder from the slope let loose, causing me to sit up in terror as I waited for it to crush us. But the worst problem was my throat. By morning it felt like I had a hard-boiled goose egg lodged in it.

With all my tossing and turning and peeing, I don't imagine that Sun-jo got much sleep, either, but he didn't complain.

On a bright note, the morning was as mild as the previous morning, and Holly was much improved. She managed to walk to the mess tent to have breakfast with us. (The night before, Zopa had served her dinner in her tent.)

The herders and yaks left an hour before we did. They would go straight up to ABC without stopping at Camp Two, which should give you some idea of the kind of shape they were in compared to us.

JR came up as I was packing the tent and said he wanted to do an interview with me before we headed up. Sun-jo and Zopa were packing up Holly's gear.

I had already done several of these interviews down at Base Camp and I dreaded doing any more. I had discovered that a camera in my face and a microphone boom dangling above my head turned me into a babbling idiot.

"Just act natural," JR would say. "Be yourself."

Right.

Then he would give me little prompts like: "What's it feel like to be up on the world's greatest mountain with your dad?" Or: "How does being up on Everest compare to climbing skyscrapers?"

I would try to answer the questions with straightforward honesty and end up spewing forth the most incredibly lame answers imaginable.

I stopped packing and joined the crew, trying not to look too glum. They had positioned the camera in front of the rotting slope, and I was up all night listening to the slope belch boulders. Will made me squat, pulled the hood off my head so they could see my face, and wiped off all my glacial cream, which I had just carefully applied.

"Man, wouldn't it be great if one of those big boulders let loose while we're doing this?" Jack said. (He was the sound guy and was always hoping that something horrible would happen when the film was rolling.)

"Okay," JR said. "We're going to keep it real simple today. I just want you to repeat what you said yesterday about the yaks and porters. That was really poignant. And you were absolutely right. I don't know if they'll use it in the final version but they sure ought to."

I was thrilled. In fact, during my sleepless night I had thought about what I said and wished they'd had the camera rolling.

JR gave the cue. "On three . . . two . . . one . . . tape rolling . . ."

I opened my mouth and nothing came out.

"We're rolling," JR said impatiently. (The camera batteries didn't last very long in cold weather.)

I tried again, but nothing came out.

"Any time, Peak."

"A boulder's coming loose," Jack said excitedly.

"Come on, Peak!"

I pointed to my mouth and shook my head. My voice was gone.

JR swore.

"That boulder's ready to pop," Jack said. "I think it's going to miss us, but it will definitely be in the frame."

"Zopa!" JR yelled. "Can you come over for a little stand-up?"

Zopa shook his head and pointed at Sun-jo. "Let Sun-jo do it."

"Get out of the frame, Peak!" JR shouted.

I moved and Sun-jo quickly stepped into my place.

"We're still rolling," JR said. "Talk about your feelings toward the mountain, Sun-jo. Maybe something about your father. On three . . . two . . . one . . ."

"My father came to Sagarmatha when he was my age," Sun-Jo said in his cool accent. "He started as a porter and worked his way up to become a Sherpa and an assistant sirdar. He told me that he climbed mountains so I would not have to, but I think there was more to it than this . . ."

The boulder Jack hoped would fall did, along with a ton of other debris. Sun-jo did not flinch, or even glance behind him at the mini-avalanche. He just kept talking, and JR kept filming.

"My father was a stranger to me, but here on the mountain I am getting to know him through the conversations of the Sherpas and climbers and porters. I came here to see the mountain, but what I'm discovering is my father."

"Beautiful!" JR said.

It *was* beautiful. And I hate to admit it, but I was a little jealous of Sun-jo's smooth performance. Unlike me, he was totally comfortable in front of the video camera. JR had never praised me after a taping. Of course I was lousy at it, but still . . .

Jack and Will were patting Sun-jo on the back, telling him what a natural he was. I walked back to our tent and finished packing. I don't think they realized I had left.

AT MIDMORNING the weather turned, with gray clouds coming in from the west and a bitterly cold wind blowing down the mountain. We had to stop and put on more layers of clothes. I covered my face with a silk balaclava and wool scarf. My throat was no better, but I trudged on, one step at a time, stopping every half hour, unwinding my shroud to drink, and gagging on every gulp.

Zopa walked behind us, still carrying Holly's load and gently coaxing her up the slope as if he were her personal Sherpa or something. I didn't know if she had hired him, or promised to give money to the Tibetan monks, or if it was something else. But without him, she would have been going downhill instead of up.

It took us eight hours (half a mile an hour) to get to Camp Two. There were so many climbers there we barely had room to pitch our tents. Some of the climbers were coming down from Camp Four above ABC, some were on their way up to ABC, and some were using the site as their Base Camp, which was hard to imagine because I could barely breathe. The film crew had to set up their tents on the far side of camp from us.

The camp was at the junction of two glaciers: East Rongbuk and Beifeng. You couldn't see the Everest summit from the camp, but there was a spectacular view of three other Himalayan peaks: Changtse, Changzheng, and Lixin.

There wasn't enough room to set up the mess tent, so we were on our own for dinner.

I got the stove going while Sun-jo walked down to a glacial pond to get water. By the time he got back it had started snowing. We put the water on the stove and waited for it to boil, which was taking longer and longer the higher we climbed.

I wasn't hungry, and I don't think Sun-jo was, either, but we both knew we had to eat.

Sun-jo asked me how I was doing. I tried to answer, but all that came out was a hissing croak. It didn't bother me that I couldn't talk. What worried me more was that the sore throat might be the beginning of something worse. There was a nasty virus going through Base Camp that had everyone in an uproar. If you catch something bad enough your climb is over. As a result the teams had circled the wagons by staying in their own camps and suspiciously eyeing the approach of other climbers as if they were plague carriers. Typically, one of the porters was accused of bringing the virus to camp, as if the climbers were incapable of carrying a virus to Everest.

As we waited for the water to boil we watched Zopa set up Holly's tent, which she crawled into as soon as it was up. He then put up his own tent and started making their dinner.

"I was talking to one of the other climbers," Sun-jo said. "He told me that tomorrow will be a big test. He's been up to ABC and has spent one night up at Camp Four. He said if we make it that far we should be able to make it to the summit . . ."

I should have been paying more attention to what Sun-jo was saying, but at that moment I was having a minor crisis that had nothing to do with my sore throat. What was causing the meltdown was the fact that it had been a relatively easy day but I was a complete wreck.

You can never tell who the mountain will allow and who it will not. Zopa's words had been echoing in my brain all day—and I was betting that Peak Marcello was in the "not" crowd, right beside George with the clogged heart and Francis of the Gamow bag.

Dr. Woo had been wrong about my conditioning or else I had screwed myself up by getting dehydrated. But if that was the case, why wasn't Sun-jo suffering? I looked over at him. He was stirring the pot, chattering away like we were camped on a beach.

THE NEXT MORNING ZOPA dragged us out of our tent before dawn. There was about a foot of new snow on the ground, but it had stopped falling.

"Hard climb today," he said. "And we need to get up fast, or there won't be a place to pitch out tents. How's your throat?"

I shook my head. My voice was still gone, but I didn't feel any worse than I had the night before, which I considered a victory.

OUTSIDE CAMP we started up the Trough, a depression that sits between two rows of jagged ice pinnacles that looked like giant canine teeth. The main path was well worn and clearly marked by the yaks. Zopa warned us to stay on the path.

"If you wander off it, even to take a pee, you could be lost forever in the ice maze."

(I promise this is the last time I'm going to talk about high-altitude bodily functions. Answering a call of nature on the mountain is a huge ordeal because at that altitude you can't do anything fast and you have to take off layer after layer of clothing. It can delay your climb by a half hour or more, which can ruin your chances of getting higher because bad weather moves in so quickly. This is why you try to take care of all this before you leave camp.)

About noon we ran into the porters, yaks, and herders heading back down to Base Camp. They were still whistling and singing and I was tempted to get in line with them. I think the only thing that stopped me was that Holly had been in front of me all day long, and I wasn't about to let her get any higher up the mountain than me.

Two hours later we got our first look at ABC. Sun-jo pointed out the tiny colored tents in the distance, but the camp wasn't as close as it looked. It was three more torturous hours away. The only bright spot was that Sun-jo and I managed to pass Holly and Zopa about a hundred yards before they reached the camp.

ABC: 21,161 feet. Higher than Kilimanjaro and Mount McKinley. And I felt it. The crude camp made every other place we had stayed seem like paradise. It was situated on a pile of rubble between a glacier (that looked like it had been formed by frozen sewage) and a rotten rock wall. The ground was littered with ankle-breaking rocks and life-ending crevasses.

JR filmed our triumphant arrival. I barely had the strength even to look at the camera as I trudged by it.

There were only about six tents set up, so there was plenty of room for us to stake out an area for the team. Unlike at Base Camp, people weren't wandering around socializing. They were either too pooped to move or terrified about twisting something this close to the top.

By the time Zopa and Holly arrived, we had our tents set up and a fire going from the wood the porters had left.

"How's your throat?" Holly asked.

Sun-jo and I nearly fell off the rocks we were sitting on. This was the first full sentence she had put together since we left Base Camp, and her voice almost sounded normal. We had passed her, but she seemed in better shape than we were.

"It's . . . still . . . sore," I said with difficulty.

"I think there's a doctor up here," she said. "I'll go find him."

By the time we had her tent up she was back with the doctor in tow. He looked like he needed a doctor himself, but he examined my throat, then called Leah Krieger down at Base Camp. They decided to put me on antibiotics.

Josh came on the radio and asked me how it was going. I couldn't answer, so I turned over the radio to Holly, who gave a glowing report. Josh said they were heading up to ABC, then to Camp Four for a night and would no doubt see us on our way down.

(I should mention something about the radios here. The frequencies were wide open, and people had nothing better to do than sit in their tents and monitor the chatter. This included Captain Shek and the soldiers. As a result, everyone was careful about what they talked about, especially expedition leaders like Josh.)

The next day was basically spent lying in our tents trying to breathe, hoping that our red blood cells were doing what they were supposed to be doing. When we moved it was in slow motion, like we were on the moon. You'd get a plate of food and stare at it, thinking a couple minutes had passed, and tell yourself you should try to eat before it cooled off. . . .

Fork to mouth.

Ice cold.

Huh?

Look at watch.

Half an hour?

How?

By the morning we left, the antibiotics had kicked in and my throat was better. I even managed to croak out a couple of understandable sentences.

Sun-jo, on the other hand, wasn't feeling good. He had spent a good deal of the night vomiting outside our tent door. Every time he puked, Zopa would come over and make him drink, worried about dehydration. I felt bad for him, but to be honest, his getting sick perked me up a little. (Terrible, I know.) I felt better knowing that I wasn't the only one having a difficult time.

The three-day trip up took us nine hours to complete on the way down. We ran into Josh between the first and second camps. He asked how my throat was, then continued toward ABC, shouting down to us that he would see us in a few days.

Holly not only carried her own backpack on the way down, she beat us to Base Camp by half an hour. *You can never tell who the mountain will allow and who it will not.*

LETTERS FROM HOME

THAT FIRST NIGHT BACK in Base Camp I slept for fifteen hours.

When I finally woke up I felt as good as I had ever felt in my entire life. I could have easily gone out for an 18,044-foot jog, but instead I walked to the mess tent and ate about nine pounds of food.

Dr. Krieger came in and watched me wolf down my last plate, then took me over to the Aid tent to look at my throat. She said that it was better, but I needed to keep taking the antibiotics for the next week to make sure it went away.

My next stop was HQ, where they congratulated me on making it to ABC and gave me a packet of letters from home. There was a card from Rolf, two letters from Mom, and five thick letters from Paula and Patrice. The envelopes were crumpled and smeared with dirt and grease. I looked at the postmarks. The mail had been sent to Josh's office in Chiang Mai, forwarded to Kathmandu, and from there, no doubt, thrown into a truck headed to the mountain.

Thin-air mail.

Getting the letters caused my good mood to tank. I hadn't spent one minute thinking about my family since I'd arrived at Base Camp, and I felt a little guilty. But what really bothered me was that the letters had arrived at Base Camp in the first place. This meant that some of those letters I had sent to my father when I was a kid probably had arrived, too.

He had gone into a tent at some high-altitude camp just like this, and come out with a stack of letters, which included a letter from his son.

I was so mad I wanted to run up to ABC and punch him in the goggles. Instead, I decided to finish *Moleskine #1* (which you are reading) and send it to my mom. Kind of like a long letter. I was not going to ignore my family the same way that Josh had ignored me. And it would fulfill my requirement for Vincent at GSS.

The next morning I went to the mess tent to get something to eat before getting back to the Moleskine. Sun-jo wasn't there.

"Boy very sick," the cook told me

I took a thermos of hot tea over to Sun-jo's tent. He was cocooned in his sleeping bag like a caterpillar larva with only his stocking-capped head sticking out.

"You shouldn't be here," he croaked, but I could tell he was happy to see me.

His eyes were sunken and bloodshot. And maybe it was the dim light coming through the blue nylon tent, but he looked like he had lost ten pounds since I last saw him.

I poured him a cup of tea.

"You shouldn't be here," he repeated.

"Forget it," I said. "You and I have been swapping germs for weeks. I'm immune." I put the cup to his lips, hoping I was right.

"I will be better in a few days."

Looking at him, that was hard to believe, but I said I was sure he was right.

I stopped by the Aid tent. I wasn't sure if Dr. Krieger's duties included treating kitchen help, but if they didn't I was going to talk her into it.

She was tapping away on her laptop, but stopped when I came in.

"How are you feeling today?"

"Fine, but I'm worried about Sun-jo."

She made me open my mouth and shone a light down my throat.

"Inflammation is almost gone," she said, clicking off the light. "But you need to keep taking those antibiotics, especially if you insist on visiting sick people in their tents."

"So you've seen him?" I said.

"Last night and this morning."

"And?"

"And he's sick, but he'll live."

I spent the next two days writing and managed to finish the first Moleskine on the day Josh was to return from ABC and Camp Four. When I got to the end of the notebook I wrote letters to Paula and Patrice thanking them for the artwork they had sent and telling them how I had pinned it up in my tent so it was the first thing I saw in the morning and the last thing I saw at night. I told them that I missed them so bad, I was thinking about rustling a yak and riding it back to New York.

Last, I wrote to Rolf. He had sent me a card with a photo of King Kong clinging to the Empire State Building. Inside were three one-hundred-dollar bills and a handwritten note:

Hang in there, Peak.
I miss you.
I want you home.
Love, Rolf

Not "we." *I* miss you. *I* want you home. With these two sentences he had done more for me than Josh had ever done, or could ever do.

I went over to HQ and addressed the envelopes. Sparky told me the mail would go out the following morning.

When Josh arrived late that afternoon, I didn't tell him about the Moleskine or the letters. He didn't deserve to know.

MOLES

KINE #2

SECRETS

THE MEETING WAS SECRET, held at HQ after the other climbers had all gone to sleep.

By invitation only: Josh, the film crew, Sparky, Dr. Krieger, Thaddeus Bowen, and Zopa, who had brought Sun-jo with him. (Sun-jo looked a little better, but not much.) Josh glared at him, and I thought for a moment he was going to ask him to leave, but he let it go.

"Where's Holly?"

No one seemed to know.

"We're not waiting," Josh said. He turned to Dr. Krieger. "How's Peak's health?"

"I think we might have gotten the infection with the antibiotics. As long as it doesn't migrate to his lungs he should be fine. There were three new cases of pneumonia reported in camp today. I suspect it's a secondary infection from the virus. William Blade is one of them. Everyone in his team is sick. They left this afternoon and we quarantined everything they left at their campsite."

The news about William Blade and her former entourage was going to please Holly to no end.

Josh turned to Zopa. "Can Peak make it to the top?"

I was still seriously annoyed with Josh over the letters and this was not helping. I hate it when people talk about me as if I'm not there.

Zopa shrugged. "We will have to see how he does at Camp Four. He was fine at ABC."

I wasn't "fine" at ABC, but I appreciated him saying so.

"Thanks for getting him up to ABC," Josh said. "I suppose you'll be heading back to Kathmandu."

Zopa gave him another shrug.

"What about Holly?" Josh asked.

"She's strong," Zopa said.

Josh looked a little surprised. I was, too. She was fine when she finally got to ABC, and on the way down, but I wouldn't have characterized her climb as strong. What was Zopa up to?

"It won't hurt us to get Holly to the summit," Thaddeus said. "She'll talk and write about it for the rest of her life. Good PR for Peak Experience."

"I suppose you're right," Josh reluctantly agreed. He pulled a notebook out of his pocket and flipped through the pages.

"Okay. We have ten people to get to the top, counting Peak and Holly. Out of those, six or seven have a decent chance if they hit the weather window right." He looked at Sparky. "Do you have some dates for me yet?"

"I'm looking at the week of May twenty-fifth through June fourth." Sparky looked over at Zopa. "But astrology might give us a better idea than meteorology."

"Any ideas, Zopa?" Josh asked.

Zopa shook his head. "I just look up at the sky."

This got a laugh from everyone, but I don't think Zopa meant it to be funny.

"If your weather prediction is right," Josh said to Sparky, "that doesn't give us much time." He walked to the calendar on the wall. "Peak's birthday is six weeks from today. That gives us about five weeks to get him into position for a summit attempt. And I'd like to get him up there earlier than that."

"I agree," Thaddeus said. "If something happens and Peak can't get to the summit, we might have a chance for a second try."

"Thaddeus, there won't be a second chance," Josh said. "Peak either makes it on the first try or he doesn't."

Josh was right. Second tries were virtually unheard of on Everest. If you fail you have to return to Base Camp. There's not enough oxygen at the other camps to get your strength back and recover. It takes three days to get back to Base Camp with a night at Camp Six and a night at ABC. Five days at Base Camp (longer if you're really hammered), then back up, which can take eight or nine days—all together nearly three weeks. It would be mid-June before I could make another attempt, long after my fifteenth birthday. Climbers have been stopped one hundred yards from the summit (by weather, exhaustion, or time) and have never made another attempt as long as they lived.

"Here's what I'm thinking," Josh continued. "There's a couple signed up to go to Camp Four, but they're strong enough to go a lot higher. In fact, they have a better chance of getting to the summit than most of the others on the team. If we put them on the two scratched permits it would increase our summit percentage by at least twenty percent."

"Did you talk to them?" Thaddeus asked.

"Yeah, but no promises. I wanted to discuss our options first."

"I think you should send Sun-jo to the summit," Holly said, startling all of us. Uncharacteristically, she had slipped into the tent quietly.

"Who?" Josh asked, annoyed.

"Zopa's grandson," Holly answered.

This sure got everyone's attention. We stared at Sun-jo and Zopa with our mouths hanging open. I think my mouth was open a little more than the others. Josh looked like he had been slapped in the face. Why hadn't Sun-jo told me that Zopa was his grandfather?

Sun-jo sat with his chin cupped in his hands, seemingly oblivious to our shock.

"What's your father's name?" Josh asked him.

"His name was Ki-tar Sherpa," Sun-jo answered.

"I knew him," Josh said quietly. "I didn't know he had a son." He looked over at Zopa and gave him his trademark grin. "What are you up to?"

Zopa answered with a shrug. None of us believed him. There was a lot more to this than Josh, Sun-jo, and Zopa were letting on.

Josh looked back at Sun-jo. "How old are you?"

"I'm fourteen years old," he answered.

I think we had just gotten to the main reason Zopa had agreed to leave the Indrayani temple and take me to Base Camp.

Josh was no longer grinning, nor was anyone else, especially me. I considered Sun-jo a friend. He must have known about a summit attempt back in Kathmandu. He certainly knew that Zopa was his grandfather. I should have guessed something was up when Zopa outfitted him in my climbing gear. Holly clearly had been let in on the secret, which might explain why Zopa had all but carried her up to ABC.

"When is your birthday?" Josh asked.

Sun-jo looked at Zopa, who gave him a nod.

"May thirty-first."

Six days before my birthday.

Josh was visibly relieved, but only for a second.

"How do we know that?" Thaddeus asked.

Sun-jo reached into the pocket of his (my) parka and produced a tattered piece of paper sealed in a Ziploc plastic bag. He pulled out the paper and handed it to Thaddeus.

"This is in Nepalese," Thaddeus said.

Josh took it from him and read it over. "No, it's Tibetan," he corrected, then looked back at Sun-jo. "You were born in Tibet?"

"Yes, sir," Sun-jo answered. "I was five when my father managed to get my mother and me across the border into Nepal. I am a free Tibetan."

"There is no such thing," Josh said. "How did you get back into Tibet? You certainly didn't use *this.*" He handed the piece of paper back.

"Forged documents," Zopa said.

Josh swore. "Well, your grandson isn't going to be a *free* Tibetan for long if Captain Shek finds out about the bogus papers," Josh said. "They'll arrest him. You'll probably be hauled away, too."

This explained Sun-jo's disappearing act whenever the soldiers were around.

"A summit attempt is worth the risk," Zopa commented.

Josh looked at Sun-jo for a moment, then back at Zopa. "I owe you, Zopa, but I haven't decided if Sun-jo's getting a shot at the top. And besides, we don't have enough climbing Sherpas to get three teams to the top. And that's what we're talking about. Three separate teams."

"Yogi and Yash," Zopa said.

Josh laughed and shook his head. "You had this all figured out before you left Kathmandu, didn't you?"

Zopa didn't answer, but it was clear he had.

"Maybe you and I should go someplace a little more private to talk about this," Josh suggested.

"That is up to you," Zopa said. "But I don't mind speaking about it here."

"Suit yourself." Josh looked at everyone in turn but lingered when he got to Holly. "This is totally off the record. Nothing we say here is to leave this tent—and I mean ever. If the Chinese get wind of this they could shut down our expedition—but worse, they might grab Sun-jo and put him in prison."

I thought of the shackled road gang we had passed after we crossed the Friendship Bridge and gave an involuntary shudder. I was mad at Sun-jo, but I didn't wish that on anyone. Being arrested in the U.S. was nothing like being arrested in Tibet. I looked at him. He seemed worried, almost as if it had just dawned on him what would happen if Captain Shek caught him with false papers.

Everyone nodded in agreement, although I think the film crew would have loved to have their camera rolling. (Not that Josh would let them use any of the footage in the final documentary.)

"Sun-jo's mother was born in a small village on this side of the mountain," Zopa explained. "My son met her on an expedition. It took him years to get her and Sun-jo out of Tibet into Nepal. Sun-jo is both Tibetan and Nepalese."

"The Chinese won't see it that way if Sun-jo gets caught up here," Josh said.

"If we put him on the summit they'll never give us a climbing permit for the north side again!" Thaddeus shouted. "That could take away half our business. The Tibet route is harder than the Nepal route. It has more prestige. By bringing Sun-jo here you've jeopardized our entire season. And for what? If Peak and Sun-jo make it to the top, Sun-jo still won't be the youngest to reach the summit."

"But he would be the youngest free Tibetan to summit," Zopa pointed out. "It's a matter of national pride."

"We're in business," Thaddeus said. "Not politics."

"What is the difference?" Zopa said.

"Enough," Josh said. He looked over at JR. "How's the filming going?"

"Okay," JR answered. "We have some decent climbing sequences, a couple of good interviews."

I cringed a little hearing this. He couldn't be talking about the interviews with me.

"Any footage of Sun-jo?"

"A lot. He and Peak have been climbing together. What are you thinking?"

"Yeah," Thaddeus added a little belligerently, "what *are* you thinking?"

"I'm not sure yet," Josh said. He looked over at me. "How do you feel about sharing the glory?"

"You've gotta be kidding me," Thaddeus said.

Josh ignored him. "What do you think, Peak?"

I wasn't doing this for the glory. Or was I? I looked over at Sun-jo and Zopa. They were both stone-faced. I was furious with both of them—Sun-jo more than Zopa because Zopa never told anybody anything.

I wanted to tell Josh to send Sun-jo packing back to Nepal, but instead, without much enthusiasm, I said, "It's okay with me."

"Can I talk to you, Josh?" Thaddeus asked. "Alone."

"Sure."

After they left everyone sat there for a few moments without saying anything. JR finally broke the silence.

"Poker?" He pulled a deck of cards out of his parka.

"Might as well," Sparky said. "Josh and Thaddeus could be a while."

"I'm in," Holly said.

I walked over to where Sun-jo and Zopa were sitting.

"Thank you for supporting me," Sun-jo said.

"You should have told me."

"I did," Sun-jo said, glancing at Zopa guiltily. "At least indirectly."

"What are you talking about?"

"Our first night at ABC," he answered. "I talked about how if *we* got up to Camp Four *we* had a good chance at the summit."

He was right about it being indirect. I barely remembered the one-sided conversation. "That's pretty lame," I said.

Zopa came to his defense. "Sun-jo did not know in Kathmandu," he said. "He thought I was taking him here to become a Sherpa. It wasn't until we were on our way to ABC that I told him about the summit."

So Josh and I weren't the only ones Zopa played cagey with. I glanced over at the poker game, which was in full swing, with a pile of money in the center of the table. They were lucky Zopa wasn't playing.

"I'm going over to the mess tent for some tea," Zopa said.

I waited until he was out of the tent, then asked Sun-jo why he hadn't told me that Zopa was his grandfather.

"Zopa thought it best if we kept that to ourselves," he answered.

If Zopa asked me to keep something to myself I probably would have, too, but it still bothered me that Sun-jo didn't tell me.

Zopa returned with a thermos of tea and several mugs. I took my mug over and watched them play poker. I wasn't really interested in the game, but I didn't want to hang with Zopa and Sun-jo. Holly won every hand, much to everyone's annoyance.

About twenty minutes later Josh and Thaddeus came back into HQ. At first I thought Thaddeus had gotten his way because he was all smiles. Sun-jo noticed his expression, too, and looked disappointed.

"All right," Thaddeus said, smiling at Sun-jo and Zopa. "You've got your shot at the summit."

"You're all heading back up to ABC the day after tomorrow," Josh added.

The film crew groaned.

BEAR AND BULL

THREE TEAMS: A, B, AND (SHH!) C.

We were the C team: Sun-jo, me, the film crew, and Holly—led by Zopa, Yogi, and Yash. (I guess the brothers had not hitched a ride to find a job on the mountain. They already had a job. Zopa had hired them to help him get Sun-jo to the summit.) And I think the C stood for "covert," not third, because we were getting the first summit shot, not the last, and somehow we were supposed to keep all of this quiet.

The night before, Josh and Thaddeus hadn't told us to outright *lie* to the other climbers, but they came pretty close to it.

"We'll have to keep this to ourselves," Thaddeus had said, lowering his voice despite the fact that it was ten degrees below zero outside and the wind was howling down the mountain at about twenty-five miles an hour. It wasn't likely someone was standing outside the flap eavesdropping.

"Thaddeus is right," Josh agreed. "Some of the other climbers are real head cases. There'll be a fight over who goes first. It's ridiculous, but it's the same every year. They can't get it into their oxygen-starved brains that reaching the summit has nothing to do with the order you climb. It depends on the weather."

Josh was fudging this a little. Sitting at Base Camp, or up at ABC waiting your turn, increases your chances of catching a virus or twisting an ankle, to say nothing of the sheer boredom and psychological damage of lying in your cramped tent day after day wondering if you are going to make it to the top.

We were getting the first shot because of my birthday. Period. It could take every one of those thirty-plus days to get me to the top before I turned fifteen.

"In case anyone asks," Thaddeus said, "this is what we're doing." He looked at the film crew. "You're making a documentary about Sherpas." He looked at Holly. "You're writing a story about Sherpas." He looked at me. "You're just tagging along to help with the filming. As far as anyone knows, a summit attempt is not part of the documentary."

"Sun-jo's going to have to move to the porter camp tonight," Josh said. "It's the only way we can keep him under wraps. Can you arrange that, Zopa?"

Zopa nodded.

Josh looked at Sun-jo. "Captain Shek and the soldiers rarely go to the porter camp, but just to be safe, you need to dress and act like a porter. No fancy western climbing clothes. The porters are hauling supplies up the mountain the day after tomorrow. You'll all go with them. When you get to Intermediate Camp, out of sight of the Chinese, you can change into your climbing gear. When you come back down you'll need to change your clothes and stick with the porters. If Shek catches you, you're toast."

"Toast?" Sun-jo asked.

"You'll be chipping boulders into gravel," I explained.

"Oh." A look of dread crossed Sun-jo's usually calm and cheerful face.

"So," Josh continued, "Zopa will lead the C team. I'll lead the A team. And Pa-sang will lead the B team."

I was disappointed that I wouldn't be trying for the summit with my father, but I wasn't surprised. ("Change of plans" had been the theme of our relationship my whole life.) I was also worried about Zopa and Sun-jo.

"Paranoia feeds on thin air . . ." That's a direct quote from one of Josh's climbing books, and the feeling was beginning to gnaw at my guts.

With Sun-jo in the mix it seemed to me that he and Zopa had everything to gain if I didn't make it to the summit. I'm not saying that they would try to stop me, but even the slightest mistake, accidental or intentional, could end my climb. And no one would be the wiser. Bad things happen on mountains. It's part of every climb. And when something goes wrong it's usually blamed on bad equipment, bad weather, bad luck—rarely on the climbers themselves.

"Any questions?" Josh asked.

I had a couple dozen questions, like: If Zopa could get forged papers good enough to get Sun-jo over the Friendship Bridge, why should we trust his tattered birth certificate? He could be six months younger than me for all we knew. Zopa knew exactly when my birthday was. He was there when Mom radioed Josh on Annapurna.

Was Josh hedging his bets by sending Sun-jo up with me? If I didn't make it, Josh's company would still receive the credit for getting the youngest climber to the top of Mount Everest. Sun-jo was on his climbing permit. Did it really matter to Josh which of us made it to the top?

But I didn't ask questions or even make a comment. I was so confused and mad, I didn't trust myself to open my mouth.

"There's no way we'll be able to keep this a secret from the other climbers," JR said. "There's only one final approach to the summit and we'll all be taking it, single file like ants."

Josh gave him the grin. "No worries. Once the A and B teams get to Camp Four the only thing they'll be thinking about is where their next breath is coming from."

"What about when they get back to Base Camp?" JR asked.

"If they get to the summit they won't care who made it to the top and who didn't," Josh answered. "The important thing is to give them a good chance. Your team will be four or five days ahead of A and B. When you get above Camp Four be careful what you say on the radio. One slip of the tongue and everyone on this side of the mountain will know what we're up to. When you pass us on your way down don't say anything about the summit. We'll sort it out later."

"The other climbers are done with their second trip to ABC," JR persisted. "They're at least a week ahead of us in terms of acclimatization."

He was right. The third trip to ABC was when you usually tried for the summit. We were a trip behind Josh's other climbers.

"If the weather breaks our way we'll try to get them to the top sooner," Josh said. "If not, they'll have to wait it out in Base Camp along with everyone else. We can't all head to the top at the same time. There isn't enough room."

Which meant the other climbers could be sitting at Base Camp for another six weeks before getting their shot at the summit. And I knew that would not *sit* well with them.

I HAD A LOUSY NIGHT lying in my sleeping bag, thinking of all the ways Zopa and Sun-jo could sabotage my summit try if they wanted to. It was a depressingly long list.

Late the next morning when I finally poked my head out of my tent, a light snow was falling. I got dressed and went over to the mess tent, where I found Zopa and the film crew talking quietly about the shift in the documentary.

(Or were they talking about me until they saw me walk up? Josh was sure right about that thin-air paranoia thing.)

"Are you sick again?" Zopa asked.

Don't you wish, I thought, but told him that I had never felt better in my life. He didn't look like he believed me. I dished up a bowl of oatmeal, then took a seat at the table next to them. We had the tent to ourselves except for the cook cleaning up after the breakfast rush.

"As soon as you finish eating," JR said, "I'll show you how to use the camera."

"Why?"

"Because there's a decent chance that Jack, Will, and I won't make it to the summit. Someone has to get it on film."

They were all strong climbers. It hadn't occurred to me that they might not make it to the top.

"We'll try," Jack said, "but you never know."

"This is my third trip to Everest," JR said. "The closest I've gotten was just above Camp Six. The weather turned us back and that was it. I'll give you one of our minicameras." He looked at his watch. "We'll meet you and Zopa outside HQ in fifteen minutes, then head over to the porter camp to shoot some footage."

They got up and left the tent.

I looked at Zopa. "Have you seen Josh?"

"He took some of his team up the mountain to practice climbing techniques."

I must have looked a little annoyed because Zopa studied me for a moment, then said, "How do you feel about your father now that you have spent time with him?"

"I haven't really spent much time with him," I answered, dodging the question.

Zopa sipped his tea, then said, "He can't help himself, you know."

"What do you mean?"

"In climbing he has found something he is very good at, something he has a passion for. Not many men find that."

"But what do you do when you get too old to climb mountains?"

Zopa laughed. "Most climbers do not get old."

"You did."

"I stopped climbing."

"Why?"

"My children were grown. I no longer needed the money."

"You must have climbed for more than money."

"Of course, but if I wasn't paid I would not have climbed at all. You climb for sport; Sherpas climb to support their families."

"So you're here to help Sun-jo become a Sherpa," I said.

"No. I'm here so Sun-jo does not have to become a Sherpa."

"What do you mean?"

"I know you're angry at me for not telling you about my plan for Sun-jo. And you're upset with Sun-jo for not telling you that I am his grandfather."

"What does that have to do with your not wanting Sun-jo to become a Sherpa?"

"To get him this far there were things I had to keep to myself. Things I asked Sun-jo to keep to himself. He really didn't know what I had in mind until I told him at ABC. I could not tell him until I saw how he did on the mountain. If he makes it to the summit, the notoriety it brings him will allow him to go back to school. I'm hoping he never has to climb again."

"Is that birth certificate real?"

"Yes. Sun-jo is a week older than you."

"What if I make it to the summit, too?"

Zopa shrugged.

This was not the answer I was hoping for. "I know what you're thinking," I said. "You can never tell who the mountain will allow and who it will not."

Zopa smiled and got up from the table. "I'll see you over at HQ."

"I'm going to make it to the summit," I told him as he walked out of the mess tent.

In a strange way the conversation helped to center me. It reminded me that climbing, even though there might be other people in your party, is a solo sport. Your legs, your arms, your muscles, your endurance, your will are yours alone. A partner can encourage you, maybe even stop you from falling, but they can't get you to the top. That's entirely up to you.

I finished my breakfast feeling a little better and walked over to HQ to meet the film crew. Zopa was there, but Holly wasn't.

"She's already over at the porter camp," JR explained. "Dr. Krieger had some meds for Sun-jo, but didn't want to take them to the camp herself. Captain Shek would find that suspicious. Doctors do not treat porters. Holly took them over for her."

I guess I wasn't the only one being transformed by the mountain. Holly had undergone a remarkable change since we got up to ABC. And it was clear by JR's attitude that I wasn't the only one to notice. Her voice was still a little shrill and she still wore her garish clothes, but she had taken care of me at ABC and now she was looking after Sun-jo. I don't think she would have done that the first day she got to Base Camp.

JR handed me a small camera about the size of a sandwich. "I know it doesn't look like much," he explained. "But it's reliable at high altitudes and it takes pretty good video—not as good as the one we've been using, but hauling the big unit to the summit is a pain in the ass."

He showed me how to zoom in and out, how to frame a shot, how to use the built-in microphone, and how to change the memory card, which held about an hour of video.

"You have to be pretty close to pick up a voice," Jack explained. "Especially if the wind's blowing. Whoever's talking will probably have to shout."

"Consider the camera yours until the climb is over," JR said. "We have another one we'll take to the top if we make it that far. You need to practice with it. The hardest part is hitting the little buttons with gloves on. So practice with gloves. If you take off your gloves above Camp Five your fingers will fall off and you'll be pushing buttons with your nose for the rest of your life."

Pleasant thought.

"What am I supposed to be filming?" I asked.

"The story," Will said.

"What story?"

"That's the big question," JR answered. "And part of the fun."

"And the mystery," Jack added.

"Josh hired us to film you," JR continued. "Now Sun-jo's been added to the mix, which changes the story. If you and Sun-jo don't make it to the summit the story will shift again. It might be about how you didn't make it—what stopped you. It might be about the friendship between you two . . ."

(Which was pretty shaky at the moment, but I didn't tell JR that.)

". . . or Sun-jo and Zopa, or you and your father. The point is that we won't know what the story is about until we know how the story ends. All we can do now is film details. When we get done we'll piece the documentary together like a jigsaw puzzle."

Which is exactly how Vincent at GSS taught me to put a story together. He wouldn't let me write a word until I'd finished my research. *Hold the story inside until you are ready to burst.*

He made me write my research notes on three-by-five cards. On each card was a scene, a character note, or a detail from my research.

When you do your research write down whatever interests you. Whatever stimulates your imagination. Whatever seems important. A story is built like a stone wall. Not all the stones will fit. Some will have to be discarded. Some broken and reshaped. When you finish the wall it may not look exactly like the wall you envisioned, but it will keep the livestock in and the predators out.

(I wondered if Vincent would accept a documentary in place of a Moleskine, but I doubted it.)

"It would be great," JR continued, "if you could write

down your shots. It's not easy to do, especially at high altitudes, but it would help us when we edit."

"If you can't write them down," Jack suggested, "you can record what you're doing on the microphone."

FROM A DISTANCE the porter camp looked neat and prosperous, but as we got closer it became clear that it was neither. It seemed that everything in it was made out of castoffs—as if the porters hung around after the climbing season and collected the leftovers from our camp and put it in theirs. There were a couple of shacks that had more flattened tin cans nailed to them than wood. The tents were sewn together from bits and pieces of other tents. The yak halters were made from frayed climbing ropes.

The camp had a different smell to it as well: dung, woodsmoke, and the old palm oil that the porters cooked their food in. But the smell and disarray were soon forgotten in the minor stampede of men that came running when they saw Zopa. Sun-jo and Holly came out of a battered tent and joined us. Sun-jo still looked pretty weak, which I wasn't unhappy to see. I wondered how he was going to do tomorrow when we headed back up to ABC.

He pulled me to the side. "I appreciate your standing up for me last night," he said. "I am sorry I didn't tell you about Zopa."

"Forget it," I said, although I hadn't come close to forgetting it myself. "How was it staying here last night?"

"It's not as comfortable as the climbing camp, but the porters have been kind."

The porters had lined up in a long row and Zopa was walking down the line greeting each in turn and giving blessings. When he finished we sat down in a large circle on blankets and sleeping bags and talked, with Zopa translating.

A good way to understand what the porters do for a living is to think of them as Himalayan truckers. The only difference is that their trucks have legs instead of wheels and are fueled by grass instead of diesel.

The nearest restaurant to our cabin in Wyoming was a truck stop. Mom and I used to go there all the time and we loved it. The truckers were friendly, funny, and full of stories. It was no different with the porters. I got so involved in their stories, I completely forgot about using my camera.

The porters were from all over Tibet and Nepal and spent nine months out of the year away from home. When they weren't hauling gear up Everest and other mountains they were guiding trekkers or moving supplies at lower altitudes. Most of the younger porters wanted to become climbing Sherpas because the money was better. The older porters seemed satisfied driving their yaks in spite of the hardships. They told us stories about falls and getting lost, but the most grim story was related at the end of the day by an old porter named Gulu, who was from the same village where Sun-jo was born.

(Gulu knew Sun-jo's mother well and claimed to have taken Sun-jo on his first yak ride when he was a baby. The porters and Sherpas were spread out over thousands of barren miles, but there always seemed to be connections like this between them.)

On the way back to camp JR said that Gulu's story was compelling but he couldn't use it in the final documentary. No room. Which is why I include it here. (Vincent taught me that what makes a story unique is not necessarily the information in the story but what the writer chooses to put in or leave out.)

WHEN GULU was a young man he bought a beautiful yak bull from a distant village. It had taken him three years to save the money for the bull, which he planned to use to increase the size of his small herd.

"It was a long distance to the village where the yak was being sold," Gulu said, shaking his gray head. "The Chinese soldiers were everywhere, and it was dangerous on the road. I traveled at night and hid in the hills during the day so they did not rob or kill me."

It took him so long to get to the village that he was afraid the bull would be gone when he got there—either sold to another buyer or killed by the soldiers for food.

"But the bull was there," he said, "and more magnificent than I remembered. His hair was as dark as a moonless night, his back was as straight as a floor timber and as broad as I am tall." He laughed. "The owner regretted the price we had agreed upon and tried to raise it."

They argued for three days. In the end Gulu gave the owner all the money he had and a promise to bring him the first two calves the bull produced the following year.

"All of this took too long," Gulu explained. "The weather had turned bad. To complicate things I now had a yak with me that had been pastured for over a year with very little exercise. He was weak in the legs from being penned. I had to stop often for him to rest and eat. The other difficulty was that I had no money and I myself had to scavenge for food."

He decided the only way he would make it home before he and the yak starved was to take a shortcut through the mountains. He had heard about the shortcut but had never traveled it.

"At first the route was good. It was far enough from the roads so that I could travel during the day without fear of soldiers. Then the path started to rise. The weather worsened the higher we climbed. The snow was deep. I should have turned back . . ." He grinned and shrugged. "But I was young and foolish and I continued to climb, driving the bull before me."

They reached the shortcut's summit and started down the other side, Gulu confident now that he and the bull were going to make it home safely. But as he was looking for a place to sleep an avalanche roared down the mountain and buried him alive.

"I was so cold," Gulu said with a shudder. "More cold than I had ever been in my life, before or since. I remember thinking how unfair it was that the avalanche hadn't killed me when it struck. I waited for death in that cold dark place, wondering how long it would be. After a while I felt a tugging on my right arm like a fish nibbling on bait. At first I didn't know what it was, then I remembered the bull. When we reached the summit I had put a rope around his neck to keep him close. It wasn't a long rope, two meters, maybe a little shorter. He was close, and he was alive, but was he above me or below? The snow was so tight around me I didn't know if I was facedown or faceup. I could have been standing on my feet for all I knew, or upside down on my head."

We all laughed, but being buried alive isn't funny.

"I am not sure why," Gulu continued, "but it seemed important to reach the bull. To touch him one last time. To apologize for taking him from the safety of his pasture. I started to pull myself along the rope. It was slow and painful work. The farther I got up the rope, the harder the yak pulled—sometimes smashing my face into the ice before I could clear it away. Perhaps the bull is free, I thought, standing on the surface, tethered by the man beneath. I finally broke through, gasping for breath. The bull *was* on the surface, but he was not standing.

"As I examined him he kicked me several times, but I was so numb I barely felt it. My beautiful bull had two broken legs. I felt shards of bone sticking through his flesh. There was only one thing to do. I unsheathed my knife and cut his throat."

The bull took a long time to bleed out. Gulu watched with tears freezing to his cheeks. Three years of hard work and sacrifice lay at his feet bleeding into the snow.

"But there was no time for sorrow," he told us. "I had to get back to my village. If I didn't, my family would have to pay the debt of the two calves. But first I had to survive the night."

He slit the yak open, pulled his guts out onto the snow, then climbed into the body cavity to warm himself.

"Early the next morning my sleep was interrupted by a violent shaking. I thought the yak was slipping down the mountain. I put my head outside the carcass, and I don't know who was more surprised: I or the bear pulling my precious bull down the mountainside.

"It reared up on its hind feet and let out a heart-stopping bellow that shook every bone in my body. I was certain I would be eaten. But I was saved by the Chinese army."

Four soldiers had been tracking the bear and caught up

to it just as it bellowed. They fired and missed, but the bullets were enough to frighten the bear away. It lumbered up the slope and disappeared into the trees.

"All I had to do now was contend with the soldiers," Gulu said. "But I didn't think this would be a problem. I had no money. If they wanted the yak for food they were welcome to it.

"As they reached the carcass, I crawled out from my bloody shelter. When they saw me, the soldiers screamed like frightened children and threw down their rifles. Before I could speak they ran away."

After Gulu returned home he heard a rumor about four soldiers coming across a yeti feeding on a yak. A few weeks later there was a story about a cow giving birth to a full-grown man.

"How did you pay for the calves?" JR asked.

Gulu smiled. "I sold the soldiers' rifles. There was enough money to pay for the calves and to buy a new bull. He was not nearly as magnificent as the one that gave birth to me, but he was a good breeder and increased my small herd tenfold."

CAMP FOUR

ZOPA ROUSED HOLLY AND ME out of our tents at sunrise. Another beautiful day: clear, crisp, twenty-two degrees and rising—which meant we'd have to pack our cold weather gear on our backs instead of wearing it. To make things worse, Zopa gave each of us a pile of Sun-jo's gear to haul up to the first camp.

Holly's share was a lot smaller than my share. She finished repacking quickly and left for the mess tent. It took me forty-five minutes to reorganize what I'd packed the night before. I was slowed down by my ill feelings toward Sun-jo and Zopa. I couldn't believe it. Not only had Zopa taken my gear and given it to Sun-jo, but now I had to haul it up the mountain for him. It seemed that he was doing everything in his power to make sure I was too weak to get to the top.

When I finally finished my pack was fifteen pounds heavier than it was for my first time up to ABC. Not good. One pound can make a huge difference at this altitude. I was trying to decide what to leave behind when Captain Shek walked up.

"You try for summit?" he demanded.

He was out of uniform, dressed like a climber, which is probably why I didn't notice him sneaking up on me.

"Not today," I said.

"How old you?"

He must have been watching and had waited to catch me alone like this.

"How old you?" he repeated aggressively.

Trick question. He'd seen my passport. He knew exactly how old I was. He wanted me to lie. I told him the truth.

"Where other boy?"

Uh-oh.

"Who?" I'm a terrible liar.

"Boy you climb mountain with last week. Boy you walk with in camp. You and he good friends."

Captain Shek's English was a little rough, but the sarcasm was crystal clear. He had watched us walking around camp. He had seen us head up the mountain to ABC.

"Oh, him," I said stupidly. "I haven't seen him in a couple days."

"Where he go?"

I shrugged.

"You lying to me!"

(Apparently I couldn't even shrug a lie.)

"I kick you off mountain if you lie."

"Go ahead," I said, zipping my pack closed. Probably not the brightest thing to say, but I'd had about enough of Captain Shek and everything else on Everest.

He looked like he was about to explode. I don't think he was used to having a fourteen-year-old call his bluff. He raised his arm, and for a second I thought he was going to hit me, but then he smiled as if he realized the "This is the People's Republic of China, you have no rights" thing wasn't going to work with me.

"What is other boy's name?" he asked in a much more reasonable tone.

"He didn't say." I picked up my pack.

"I watching you."

I walked away feeling his eyes drilling into the back of my neck, proud of myself for not even thinking about ratting out Sun-jo.

As soon as I found Zopa I told him about the conversation. He was a lot calmer about it than I was, saying that Captain Shek was the least of our problems.

"In a few days you will be at Camp Four," he said. "This is all you need to worry about."

It turned out that he was right.

WE JOINED A SMALL GROUP of porters and their yaks heading up the mountain. Sun-jo was not with them. When I asked Zopa about this he said, "He will be along."

The trip up to Intermediate Camp was a lot easier than the first time. I wasn't able to sing and chant with the porters, but I was able to talk as I walked, which was a big improvement. I even managed to use the tiny video camera and discovered that I was a lot more comfortable behind it than I was in front of it.

The landscape had changed dramatically from the previous week. The warm weather had created several new streams of glacial runoff. It was difficult to find places to cross without drenching ourselves. The other problem was the rocks. The thaw was causing them to pop loose from the ice. It was like the glacier was a bowling lane and we were the pins. One of the porters and his yak got hit by a large rock and had to return to Base Camp.

"Did you get the strike on tape?" Jack asked.

"Uh, no."

He swore.

I spent most of the trip with Holly, who wasn't doing that well (I think because she was carrying her own pack). I offered to lug it for a while, but she insisted on carrying it herself (for which I was relieved).

She said she was thinking about heading home after we got down from Camp Four and wanted to know if I would give her an exclusive interview after I got down from the summit.

"You're going to quit?"

"Reaching the summit of Everest was not on my to-do list this year. If it had been, I might have done some practice climbs and visited the gym a little more leading up to this. Or maybe even climbed a skyscraper or two." She grinned and pointed at the peak. The clouds had cleared enough for us to see the very top. "I don't know if you've noticed, but that's one of the most daunting sights on earth."

"You don't strike me as easily daunted."

"Yeah, well . . ." She took a deep breath. "I've learned a couple things about myself up here. One, I'm getting older. And two . . ." She took another deep breath. "This mountain is a lot bigger than I am. It's humbling. The truth is I've had time to do some thinking. I can't tell you how long it's been since I've been alone. That's been humbling, too. Pierre and Ralph taking off was probably the best thing that ever happened to me."

Being in a camp with over three hundred people is not exactly being alone. But I knew what she meant. You don't have to be alone to feel alone.

"What about that interview?" she asked again.

I'd been doing some thinking, too. "We'll see," I said.

I could tell that Holly wanted to argue, but she was too out of breath to pursue it.

She and I straggled into camp after everyone else and we were both surprised to see Sun-jo sitting on a rock with a cup of hot tea in his hands, looking a little rumpled in his porter clothes.

"When did you get here?"

"A half hour ago."

"You left ahead of us?"

"No," he said, "I left the same time that you left."

I thought he was pulling my leg. There had been a dozen or so porters and maybe half that number of yaks. I couldn't have missed him.

"I rode on Gulu's yak."

"Yeah, right," I said. "When you were a baby." I had walked with Gulu some on the way up. The only thing I'd seen on his yak's back was a pile of hay.

"No," Sun-jo insisted. "I was concealed beneath the hay."

"You're kidding?"

He shook his head. "It was hot and uncomfortable."

I told him about Captain Shek.

A worried look crossed his face. "That means I'll have to go up the mountain again on the yak. I'm not looking forward to that. Thank you for carrying my things up here."

I wished he wasn't always so polite. It would be easier to be mad at him. "No problem," I said, and realized that the extra weight hadn't been a problem. That was encouraging.

I looked around camp. It had not improved in the past week. The boulder-belching slope looked even more unstable than the last time we had been here. Zopa was looking at the slope, too, shaking his head.

"We cannot camp here tonight," he said. "We will go farther up."

I didn't recall anywhere to camp farther up, and I was right. He stopped us about a thousand feet above the collapsing wall and had us carve sleeping platforms into the ice. It took hours, and it was exhausting work at that altitude, but I was happy to do it. Anything was better than sleeping under the wall.

The next morning the cold was back, which was good because it lessened the chances of avalanches. On the way to Camp Two we heard over the radio that there were three climbing parties moving up to Camp Five. They were going to make a summit attempt the following day.

Gulu was concerned because they had taken only one load of oxygen tanks to Camp Five. Zopa radioed Josh.

"I heard," Josh said. "Idiots. None of them are fully acclimated. This is only their second time above Camp Four. As far as the tanks go, some of them are going to try to get to the top without supplemental Os. So there should be enough for those who need it."

"If the weather holds," Zopa said.

"I talked to them about that, but their concern is that there won't be another good weather window. Nothing we can do about it. After they get to Camp Five they're on their own."

What he meant by this is that above Camp Five there is little chance for rescue. The air is too thin for a helicopter and at that altitude everyone is too out of it to help anyone but themselves. If you die above Camp Five your corpse stays there forever.

"Oh," Josh said, "one more thing. Captain Shek has been asking around about a Sherpa boy. Says he thinks he came up on the truck with you."

"Sun-jo," Zopa said. "He left a few days ago to go back to school. He just came up for the ride."

"I'll pass that on to the captain."

This part of the conversation was obviously completely planned for Captain Shek's benefit. The only problem now was that if the captain caught sight of Sun-jo again, Zopa was going to be in trouble, too.

"Everything else okay?" Josh asked.

"Yes. We are all fine."

"I'll check in later."

Zopa signed off and JR pointed his video camera at Zopa. "Do you think those climbers will make it to the summit?"

"Perhaps," Zopa said. "But it is too early in the season. If they make it, others will try and some of them will die. There are no shortcuts to the top of Sagarmatha."

By the time we reached ABC the following afternoon we were all exhausted, especially Sun-jo, who was still feeling the effects of his recent illness. In a role reversal from our last time at ABC, I made dinner for us while he lay in his sleeping bag. I'd like to say that I felt sorry for him, but the truth is that I didn't. I was still resentful about his horning in on my climb.

After we ate I went outside and found the porters and Sherpas sorting through the gear they were going to haul up to Camp Five.

Zopa explained that the yaks could not go much past ABC. The Sherpas would carry the gear on their backs to camps Four, Five, and Six and establish camps a few days before we made our summit attempt. In the meantime a couple of them would stay at ABC to guard our stuff.

"People would steal it?" I said.

"It has happened," Zopa said. "Not all expeditions are as well equipped or funded as your father's. Some climbers come to the mountain with nothing more than what they can carry, and sometimes they borrow equipment they find along the way."

The next morning he had us lighten our packs, carrying only what we needed for a night at Camp Four, which was a good thing because, three hours above ABC, we reached the foot of the Col, which is basically a pass between two peaks.

It was clear why the Col was a dead end for the yaks. The wall leading up to the pass was enormous. And from the base it looked terrifyingly unstable. Half of the wall was smooth, rounded off by strong winds, giving it the look of soft ice cream. The other half was made out of nasty seracs (or ice towers) that looked like giant jagged teeth. If I'd had enough breath the sight would have taken it away. I looked at my altimeter watch: 7,000 meters or 22,965 feet.

Holly slogged up and rested her hands on her knees before looking up at the terrible wall.

"No . . . *gasp* . . . way," she said.

I agreed.

Yogi and Yash walked up next, frowning and shaking their heads. Zopa and Sun-jo arrived last. Zopa was carrying Sun-jo's pack. Sun-jo looked really bad. When he saw the wall his face filled with dread. I almost felt sorry for him.

"Imagine what it was like two days ago when it was thawing," Zopa said.

It was a good point. Three teams had made it up to the Col in worse conditions than this.

The first stage was the hardest. It was up a steep pitch of soft ice. Sherpas had cut steps into the ice and there were fixed ropes, but the ice was slick and the ropes were still coated with ice because we were the first up that day.

We fell into an agonizing rhythm. *Slide the jumar up the rope.* (A jumar is a mechanical ascender with a handle that slides up the rope and grabs on so you have something to hold on to as you pull yourself up.) *Step, breathe, jumar, step*... Three hours later it was more like: *jumar, think, look up, think again, step, rest, rest, rest, hug the wall, pray*... as a chunk of ice the size of a Hummer fell past, crashing below, followed by the sound of our leaders, Yogi and Yash, laughing. Real funny. They were breaking away the loose ice along our route so it wouldn't unexpectedly peel us off the wall or knock our heads out of our butts—helmet and all.

I was next in line followed by the film crew, Holly, Sun-jo, and Zopa. The climb was anything but quiet with the brothers shouting *"Ice!"* and Zopa shouting *"Faster!"*

Four hours after we started up I reached the steepest pitch. Fifty feet. It might as well have been fifty miles. My arms and legs were numb and virtually useless, but the worst part was the air. There wasn't any. Or so it seemed. Each breath seemed to yield only a thimbleful of precious oxygen. Maybe enough to keep a bird alive, but not enough for an exhausted fourteen-year-old climber. Dr. Woo had been wrong. There was something the matter with me.

Yogi and Yash were already on top. One of them was manning the ropes and I hoped the other one was boiling snow at Camp Four. We would all need a steaming cup of tea when we got there. If we got there.

Holly, Sun-jo, and Zopa had dropped farther behind, but I could still hear Zopa shouting at them to move faster.

I was about ready to give up and head back down and go home when JR came up behind me. He looked terrible. His beard and goggles were covered with ice. It was a wonder he could see where he was going.

"Thanks for waiting," he rasped. "I need to film you arriving. Give me a couple of minutes' head start to set the shot."

I didn't have enough breath to tell him that I hadn't been waiting. I looked at my watch, and by the time I figured out what time it was, JR was already several feet above me. Without actually thinking about it I started up behind him.

An hour later, when I finally reached the top, Yogi hauled me over the edge by my backpack, which I was sure was not the shot JR wanted. Yogi's assist reminded me that seven weeks ago to the day a cop had done the same thing to me on the top of the Woolworth Building. I'd come a long way and it felt like it. I spent a good ten minutes on my knees trying to catch my breath until it dawned on me (again) that at this altitude there was no breath to catch. With difficulty I got to my feet and stumbled over to where Yash was trying to boil water.

Camp Four was tiny, and to make it worse, there was a gaping crevasse running beneath the crest, which I'd read was getting wider every year. Some believed that one of these days (hopefully not today) the whole thing would collapse and climbers would have to devise a new route up the north side.

I looked toward the summit, which was shrouded in gray mist, but I could see enough to pick out the route along the north ridge and across the north face to the pyramid. It seemed like a very long way from where Yash and I were squatting.

I couldn't imagine the three climbing parties trying for

the top feeling like I did. My ribs ached from trying to get enough Os into my lungs to survive. I knew that Zopa was carrying at least two tanks in case of emergency and I suspected that Yogi and Yash had a couple stashed as well. Sherpas do not climb without loads. For them that would be a waste of effort. I thought about begging Yash for a hit off the tank, but resisted the urge, knowing it would defeat the purpose of the climb. Instead, I started to put together my tent, which seemed a lot more complicated than it had at ABC the day before.

Jack and Will came over the top next. Will spent a good ten minutes on his hands and knees puking. (JR did not film this.)

Forty-five minutes later I was still working on the tent when Yogi hauled Holly over the edge, followed by Sun-jo and Zopa.

Zopa was shaking his head in disgust muttering, "Too slow, too slow, too slow . . ." He bent down to the two slowpokes. "If you climb like that above here you can forget the summit."

Holly and Sun-jo were out of it and didn't appear to have the slightest idea of what he was saying. I thought he was being pretty harsh considering Holly's lack of conditioning and Sun-jo's recent sickness. He came over to where I was struggling with the tent and I thought, here it comes, but instead he patted me on the back.

"You did good," he said. "You have a chance."

That was like a whole tank of Os flowing into my bloodstream. Maybe he wasn't going to try to stop me from getting to the summit.

Suddenly, the tent made complete sense. I had it together

in less than five minutes. I got everything unpacked, the pads and sleeping bags spread out, then I started in on Holly's tent as she and Sun-jo watched through dull, lifeless eyes.

The burst of energy cost me. As soon as I finished, it was all I could do to get to my feet. Zopa brought over three mugs of tea and made us drink them down.

"Get your stoves going," he said. "I know you are not hungry, but you have to eat and drink." He looked up at the sky. "It's going to snow tonight."

ARREST

ZOPA, THE WEATHER MONK, was right. Next morning: two feet of new snow.

Sun-jo and I probably didn't get three hours of sleep between us. He must have been feeling better, though, because he groggily offered to start the stove. The process sometimes takes ten or fifteen minutes because there isn't enough oxygen to keep the flame going on the gas lighter long enough to light the stove.

I crawled out with our pan to collect some snow to melt and saw Zopa, the Sherpa brothers, and the film crew were already up. And it was obvious from the steam coming off their pan of water that they had been up for quite a while. Zopa was talking on the radio. That could mean only one thing this early in the morning. Someone was in trouble. I glanced toward the summit through the swirling snow. If it was this bad down here, it was much worse up there.

"Yogi and Yash will stay here at Camp Four," Zopa was saying. "If the weather breaks they will try to get oxygen up to Camp Five."

"I'm not sure we can get them down to Camp Five," a shaky German-accented voice said.

"You must!" Zopa said forcefully. "There is no chance of rescue at Camp Five or Six. In this weather you will have to come down to Camp Four. You must leave Camp Six as soon as you can. Do you understand?"

This was followed by a long silence, then a discouraged and quiet, "*Ja, verstehe ich.*"

He understood.

Zopa gave him a blessing in Nepalese and signed off.

"Are these the same Germans you did the *puja* ceremony for?" I asked.

Zopa nodded. "The Italians are up there as well."

"What's going on?"

"Two cases of HAPE at Camp Six," JR answered. "Maybe another mild case at Camp Five. Two climbers headed up to the summit a little after midnight and haven't been heard from since."

In this weather that meant they were probably dead, or hypothermic and close to death.

"Maybe we can go up to Camp Five with Yogi and Yash and help," I said.

Zopa shook his head. "You and Sun-jo and Miss Angelo need to get down to ABC. Other Sherpas are coming up to help, but until the climbers get to Camp Five there is nothing anyone can do. As soon as you eat pack your things. We need to leave before the weather worsens."

Because of the snow and ice, getting down the Col was worse than going up—and it wasn't made any easier by thinking about the climbers dying farther up the mountain.

We passed the Sherpas coming up to help. They were loaded with oxygen bottles and Gamow bags. Their plan was to get to Camp Four that afternoon. If the weather didn't hold them back, they would head up the mountain the following morning to help Yogi and Yash get whoever had made it to Camp Five down to Camp Four. If the weather broke, a rescue helicopter might be able to get that high, but even on the best day an airlift was dicey. If the chopper couldn't make it, the Sherpas would have to get the climbers down to ABC as best they could.

We made it down to ABC in pretty good time in spite of the snow. I think what drove us was our eagerness to crawl into our tents and sleep for two days. The camp was nearly empty. Sun-jo was still pretty weak, but confident that he would be better by the time we came up. I was beginning to feel a little less surly toward him. This probably had a lot to do with Zopa's compliment the night before. I was pretty sure they weren't out to sabotage my climb.

The next morning the film crew members were all vomiting. It looked like they had caught the same thing Sun-jo had. Zopa cut their acclimatization short and arranged to have them go down to Base Camp with another climbing party. None of them complained.

"I'm going, too," Holly said.

Zopa shook his head. "You are fine. To complete the acclimatization you will need to stay here at least two days."

She gave him a smile. "It's over for me," she said. "I have no desire to go higher than Camp Four."

"You could make it to the summit," Zopa insisted.

She shook her head, and grinned. "Too slow. It's not in me this year. I appreciate all you've done." She shook his hand, then turned to me. "What about that interview after you get to the summit?"

"I may not make it to the summit," I hedged.

"I think you will." She looked at Sun-jo. "How about you? Will you give me an exclusive interview after you come down?"

"Yes."

I thought he was being overly optimistic, but I didn't say anything.

"It's a deal and your grandfather is our witness," Holly said. "It means you can't talk to any other print journalist until after you talk to me."

"Call you in New York City?"

"Yes." She wrote down several numbers. "Don't lose them."

Before she left she gave me a hug. I didn't mind this time. In fact, I was going to miss her, which surprised me.

"If you ever get back to New York, Peak, you'd better call."

"I will."

As they headed down, JR stopped and shouted back for me to remember to use the camera.

Just before dark five climbers (two Germans, three Italians) and their Sherpas stumbled into ABC looking like they had been buried alive. Most of them had frostbite someplace on their bodies—fingers, toes, ears, noses. One of them had snow blindness and had been led into camp by a rope tied around his waist.

There was no doctor in camp, so Zopa and Gulu (who had stayed behind with his yak so he could sneak Sun-jo back into Base Camp) did their best treating their injuries. When they finished it was clear that three of the climbers were not going to make it down to Base Camp on their own. The other two German climbers who had HAPE were not going to make it down at all. They had died at Camp Six two hours after Zopa talked to the distraught German climber the previous day. Four dead, assuming the two climbers headed to the summit didn't make it (which was a pretty good assumption at that point).

It's hard to think straight at that altitude, but I had enough feeling in my oxygen-starved brain to feel a little shame over the way I had been thinking about Sun-jo. Climbing Everest is not a competition. It's life and death.

The surviving climbers at Camp Six headed down to Camp Five. Yogi and Yash were helping them haul the climber with mild HAPE to Camp Four. Those who could would have to make their way to ABC the next day.

Zopa radioed Josh and told him what was going on.

"We have a chopper here with a Chinese pilot willing to take a risk," Josh said. "But the weather is going to have to get a lot better up there before he can give it a shot. Do you think it might clear before dark?"

Zopa did not have to look. Visibility was down to about twenty feet. "Negative," he answered.

"Then we'll have to wait until tomorrow. Any idea when the climbers from Camp Four will make it down to ABC?"

"No, but we will go up to meet them. Early afternoon, I hope."

"The chopper's small," Josh said. "It will hold only four people aside from the pilot and Captain Shek. You'll have to choose who gets a ride and who goes down on their own two feet."

"Captain Shek is coming up?"

"That's what I hear. He's still looking for that kid."

"Why? The boy left. He is certainly not up here."

"I told Shek that, but apparently he doesn't believe it. He searched the porter camp yesterday. And today he has soldiers checking everyone coming down to Base Camp."

"I guess he can do what he wants," Zopa said, but I could see he was worried.

So was Sun-jo. I wasn't sure how they were going to get him back down to the porter camp. Gulu's yak had eaten its hay, so there was nothing for Sun-jo to hide under. Captain Shek checking climbers was not good news, nor was his search of the porter camp.

"We have a lot of injured climbers up here," Zopa continued. "We could use the room in that helicopter."

"I know," Josh said. "I'll talk to Captain Shek again. Maybe he'll realize that taking up an empty seat might be the death of a climber, and the death would be his fault."

It was true, but the conversation was entirely for Captain Shek's benefit, who was no doubt eavesdropping.

"I hope so," Zopa said, then changed the subject. "Did Miss Angelo and the film crew get down?"

"They just arrived. Holly's packing her gear. There's a truck leaving tomorrow. To tell you the truth, she made it farther up the mountain than I expected. Doc's taking a look at the film crew right now. They barely made it into camp. Almost everybody has the virus down here. Leah's going crazy treating everyone. The chopper brought in more antibiotics. Five more climbing parties pulled up stakes this morning and left the mountain, sick as dogs. I think I'm getting it, too. If it keeps up no one is going to get to the summit from this side."

I hoped that what I'd gotten over was the same virus everyone else was getting now and that I wouldn't get it again.

I'd have to be careful when I got back down. I wasn't about to have a virus wreck my chances of getting to the summit.

EARLY THE NEXT MORNING Zopa sent everyone down to Base Camp except for the climber with snow blindness and the man with frostbitten feet. Sun-jo and Gulu went with them. Sun-jo couldn't very well stay at ABC with Captain Shek coming up. I didn't ask how they were going to get him to the porter camp, but I guessed they would keep him at one of the camps between ABC and Base Camp until Captain Shek gave up.

Zopa asked if I wanted to go, too. I did, but I told him I'd stay and help him with the climbers coming down from Camp Four.

The weather had broken during the night. It was still cold, but the clouds had thinned and the wind had died down some. The climber with mild HAPE had gotten worse during the night and they put him in a bag. This meant they would not be able to bring him down the treacherous ice wall. The chopper would have to rescue him at Camp Four.

Our job was to help Yogi and Yash get the remaining climbers and Sherpas down to ABC as quickly as possible. If some of them needed to be flown to Base Camp they had to be ready to go when the chopper landed at ABC. There would only be one flight.

WE TRAVELED LIGHT and got to the base of the Col just as Yogi was coming down. He said that Yash was staying with the injured climbers at Camp Four.

"How many?" Zopa asked.

"Three. Two with bad frostbite and the one with HAPE."

He looked up. "Some of those coming down could also use a ride to Base Camp."

There were six climbers all together, exhausted but happy to get off the wall. Zopa offered them hits of oxygen, which most of them gratefully took. No point in acclimatization now. After they got to Base Camp they would be going home.

A half hour outside ABC the chopper flew over us on its way up to Camp Four. Zopa hurried everyone along thinking the pilot would not stay long after he landed at ABC.

It turned out the stay was longer than expected.

The chopper landed ten minutes after we arrived. Zopa picked two of the most debilitated climbers for the ride down and one backup in case Captain Shek had listened to reason and stayed at Base Camp.

He hadn't.

He stepped through the miniblizzard caused by the rotors wearing a full uniform including a pistol. The pilot followed behind him and looked as unhappy as all of us did. Helicopters aren't designed to fly at that altitude. If the weather got worse it wouldn't be able to fly.

Captain Shek didn't appear to be in any hurry at all. He casually walked over to the mess tent and looked inside, then smelled the pot of stew simmering on the gas stove like he was some kind of gourmet.

"I will see everybody papers," he said.

He had to be kidding. It was one thing to check everyone coming off the mountain, but to do it at 21,161 feet with injured climbers waiting to be evacuated was outrageous. Several of the climbers let out a howl of protest despite the thin air and their condition.

"Why would we have our bloody papers up here?"

"This is an emergency! We need to get the injured to Base Camp!"

"Are you crazy?"

Captain Shek seemed a little shocked at the response, and changed his tact. "We search camp before we leave," he said, causing another vocal outburst, which he ignored.

He and the pilot went through all the tents (although the pilot was clearly not happy about the duty).

When they finished Captain Shek said, "We looking for boy."

Everyone looked at me.

"Not that boy. Nepal boy. Same age."

"He went back home over a week ago," Zopa said.

Captain Shek shook his head. "I don't think." He pointed at the chopper. "You come with me."

"We have injured climbers," Zopa said mildly. "I'll check in with you when I get to Base Camp tomorrow."

"No," Shek said. "You come with me now. I arrest you."

One of the German climbers took a step toward the captain. He was the team leader who had talked to us from Camp Six. His name was Dietrich. His face was bright red and it wasn't from the cold. He began shouting in German, which I didn't understand.

I don't think Captain Shek understood, either, but he put his hand on his pistol.

Zopa stepped in front of Dietrich and said something to him in German, then turned to the pilot and asked something in Chinese.

The pilot thought about it for a moment, then answered.

"He thinks he can take four climbers," Zopa said.

There were two additional climbers who could have used a ride, but Dietrich relaxed a little and gave a terse nod.

"What about you?" I asked Zopa.

Zopa shrugged. "It's just a misunderstanding."

He and I knew it was more than that. The question was, how much did Captain Shek know?

"I'll radio Josh and tell him what's going on."

"Be careful going down," Zopa said. "You'll have to leave early and go slow. Ask Josh to send some Sherpas up to meet you in case I'm detained longer than I expect."

Ten minutes later they took off. I radioed Josh and told him about Zopa's arrest.

"Shek's a maniac!" he shouted. "The Sherpas and porters down here are going to go nuts when they find out."

I wondered if Captain Shek's men would pass this on to him. I suspected they would. I also suspected that's exactly why Josh said it.

FAMILY HISTORY

THE NEXT DAY I expected to see Sun-jo at one of the intermediate camps, but he wasn't hiding out in either one. This meant they had figured out a way to get him down to the porter camp, or else Captain Shek had gotten his hands on him. Whatever his fate, I didn't have a lot of time to worry about it because our trip down to Base Camp was a nightmare.

Once again the weather had warmed up, turning some of the glacial rivers into raging torrents. If we'd had boats and paddles instead of crampons and ice axes we could have been down to Base Camp in minutes.

By the time we reached the first intermediate camp about half our party was ready to give up and spend another night high on the mountain.

"We should push on," Dietrich urged them. "We need to get the frostbite taken care of. We can be at Base Camp in three hours."

Unfortunately, no one else seemed to share his opinion (including the other Germans on his team, who I think blamed him for their summit failure). They sat on rocks staring at him dully as if he had lost his mind. But Dietrich was right. We were headed downhill. Even with their injuries it wouldn't take long to get to Base Camp. I knew they were tired and hurting (so was I), but spending another night at a crummy camp this close to Base was stupid. The Sherpas appeared to be behind Dietrich 100 percent. None of them had even sat down to rest.

"I think Dietrich is right," I said.

One of the Germans laughed. "Ah, now we have a child telling us what to do." Some of the others laughed with him.

Ouch. I should have kept my mouth shut. I wasn't really in a position to tell them what to do, even if I was right.

"What's the matter with all of you?" someone behind us shouted.

I turned around and was shocked to see Josh. And he wasn't alone.

"Bad weather coming in tonight," Zopa added. "You cannot stay here."

Josh was grinning, but I could tell he wasn't feeling well. His eyes were bloodshot and he looked pale and haggard. He patted Dietrich on the back. "Sorry about the trouble up on the mountain."

Dietrich looked like he was about ready to cry. I wasn't sure if it was from grief over the dead climbers or relief that Josh and Zopa had shown up to give him a hand.

Josh walked over to the sitting climbers. "If we leave right now we should be able to get down before dark. We have a team of doctors waiting to treat you. Hot food. Get up. Let's go."

No one was laughing at Joshua Wood. I remembered what my mother said about there being no one better than Josh when you are at the end of your rope. He was obviously sick, but here he was encouraging climbers who weren't even members of his own expedition.

Slowly, one by one, they started getting to their feet. Zopa took the lead with Dietrich. Josh and I followed behind.

"How was Camp Four?" he asked tiredly. "Any problems?"

"It was hard, but not as bad as I thought it would be. My ribs hurt from trying to get enough air."

"No worries. Everybody goes through it. Zopa says you're ready for the summit."

It was one thing for Zopa to give me some words of encouragement after a hard climb. It was another thing for him to tell Josh that I was ready to summit. I didn't know what to say. At that point the summit seemed like too big of a subject to tackle, and maybe even bad luck to talk about. I think Josh knew how I felt, maybe better than I did, because he didn't say any more about it. The squirt of paranoia from a few days before seemed to have evaporated.

"What happened with Zopa and Captain Shek?" I asked.

"A minirevolution. As soon as the porters and Sherpas heard about Zopa's arrest they all gathered around Shek's headquarters to hold a silent vigil. They were there when the chopper landed. Shek tried to disperse them, but they wouldn't budge. He hauled Zopa into the building, hoping to outwait them, but that didn't work. They'd still be there if he hadn't cut Zopa loose. He had no choice but to let him go."

"And Sun-jo?"

"That's the best part. Shek pulled all the soldiers back to headquarters, which made it easy to sneak Sun-jo back into the porter camp. If he hadn't detained Zopa, I'm not sure how we would have gotten Sun-jo off the mountain. He might have had to stay at one of the intermediate camps until he tried for the summit."

"Why is Captain Shek so worried about him?"

"I think he knows more about what we're trying to do than he's saying."

"How'd he find out?"

Josh shrugged. "It's hard to keep a secret up here, even if everybody keeps their mouths shut. Speaking of which . . ." He slowed down. "Your mom called."

The grin was gone. His easygoing mood had completely changed.

"Why'd you write her?" he asked.

"Because she wrote to me," I said a little more belligerently than I intended. (I guess my mood had changed, too.)

Josh looked confused.

I knew that one day I'd have this conversation with him, but I didn't think it would be at 20,000 feet with him sick and me so tired I could barely lift my feet. But I guess there is no ideal time or place for something like this.

"I thought we had an agreement," he said. "I thought we were going to let me handle your mother."

"There was no agreement," I said, and I didn't think anyone could "handle" my mother.

We glared at each other.

"The least you could have done," he said, "was to tell me that you wrote her so I wasn't blindsided."

"The least you could have done is to write me back!"

"What the hell are you talking about?"

"I sent you letters."

"You mean when you were a kid?"

"Yeah."

"So?"

"You got the letters?" I shouted.

He stopped and pulled his goggles around his neck. "Yeah, I got your letters. What does that have to do with telling your mother about Everest?"

"Everything," I said.

He didn't get it and he didn't seem to care. "Well, she's royally pissed off," he said. "It was all I could do to stop her from flying over here and yanking you off the mountain. At least I think I stopped her. She wants you to call her as soon as you get to Base Camp."

"Fine," I said.

"She insisted that I take you to the top myself, which screws up everything. I'm either going to have to go with you and Sun-jo, or you'll have to join my team. Which means there will be a long delay in your summit attempt because it looks like we'll be the last team to go. I'm in no shape to climb and neither is anyone else on the team."

"Lucky you have a backup in Sun-jo," I said. "Either way you'll get the youngest climber in the world to the summit."

"Is that what this is about?" he asked. "You're mad because it's not about just you anymore?"

"It was never about me," I said. "It's always been about you."

I walked away from him, past the injured climbers, past Dietrich, past Zopa, arriving back at Base Camp a half hour before any of them. I barged into HQ, grabbed the sat phone, and punched in the number as I stomped over to my tent. Mom answered on the first ring.

"Peak."

I got a little choked up when I heard her voice, and it was a second or two before I could respond.

"Hi, Mom."

Silence. That went on so long that I thought I'd lost the connection.

"You should have told me," she finally said.

I was tempted to say that I had told her in the Moleskine, but I knew that wouldn't fly. "Sorry," I said.

"That didn't sound very sincere, but I'll accept it. How'd you do at Camp Four?" she asked quietly.

I was shocked at how calm she was. "It was hard," I answered. "But I'm good."

"Your ribs are okay?"

"A little sore, but yeah, they're fine. You're not mad?"

"Furious."

That was more like it, but she didn't sound furious.

"Josh told me you were sick."

"I'm over it, but a lot of the others have it now." (Including Josh, but I didn't tell her that.)

"I know," she said. "Since I got your journal I've been surfing the Everest websites. Looks like a lot of climbers are leaving the mountain. I also read about the deaths at Camp Six."

"I walked down the mountain today with the German team leader," I told her. "His name is Dietrich."

"And how is he?"

"I don't know . . . devastated, I guess."

"And how are you?"

"What do you mean?"

"Well, four people died less than a mile away from you," she said, sounding a little more like my mother. "Any thoughts on that? Feelings? Reaction?"

I didn't know what to say. "I feel bad" didn't quite cut it. Mom was just getting warmed up.

"Four people died on the mountain. Human beings, Peak, with mothers, fathers, brothers, sisters, children, wives, husbands, girlfriends, boyfriends sitting at home worrying about them. By now they've gotten a phone call or an e-mail with the bad news. 'Sorry, your husband/wife/daughter isn't coming home. No, we can't retrieve a body above Camp Four. It's too dangerous . . .'"

I reached my tent and climbed inside.

"Let me ask you a question," she said.

"Go ahead."

"Do you think you're a better climber than the four who died?"

"No."

"Do you think you're luckier than they were?"

"I guess," I said. "I'm alive."

"That's not what I'm getting at."

"You're saying that the same thing could happen to me."

"You're not on the wall in back of our cabin or at a climbing camp. You're on Everest. People die up there, Peak. You might die."

"The guys who died weren't acclimatized," I protested. "They should have waited. They saw a break in the weather and got summit fever. They made a mistake."

"You think that means anything to those who were waiting at home for them?"

I looked up at the drawings that the two Peas had sent.

"Well?" Mom persisted.

One of the drawings was a stick figure clinging to a skyscraper with a helicopter hovering overhead. Just above the stick figure was a little blue mountain.

"I'm trying for the summit," I said. "I've gone through too much to give up now."

This was followed by a longer silence than the first.

"I wish you wouldn't do it, Peak, but I'm not surprised by the decision. I know what I would have said to my mother if I were on Everest getting ready for the climb of my life."

She rarely talked about her parents. They still lived in Nebraska and I had met them only twice. It wasn't much fun either time. They didn't approve of Mom, me, Josh, Rolf, or even the two Peas. Mom had left home right after high school and never lived there again.

"I'll be careful," I said.

"No one climbs a mountain thinking they're not coming back down."

"How are the two Peas?" I asked.

"You're changing the subject."

"Yeah."

Mom sighed. "Hang on a minute."

About thirty seconds later the sat phone earpiece was filled with a pair of screaming, giggling six-year-olds.

"Where are you?"

"When are you coming home?"

"I miss you!"

"No, I miss you!"

"Did you get our letters?"

"Mommy was mad at you."

"Are you coming home for our birthday?"

This went on for a while and I just listened with a big stupid grin on my face. Until I heard them, I hadn't realized how much I missed them.

Mom finally took the phone away from them. "Okay, okay," she said. "You have to let Peak answer your questions. I'm going to put him on speakerphone. You two are going to sit there quietly. If you make one sound, the phone call's over."

I heard a click.

"I miss you, too," I said. "I'm on a big mountain called Everest. In a country called Tibet. I have your drawing hanging up in my tent. I'm looking at it right now. I'm not sure if I'm going to be there for our birthday or not. I have to get to the top of the mountain first—"

"Can I ask, Mommy?" Patrice asked.

"Yes, but only one question. Then Paula can ask a question. Then you both need to go back to the kitchen and finish breakfast or you'll be late for school."

"But—"

"No." Mom cut her off. "One question each, then back to breakfast. Do we have a deal?"

The twins reluctantly agreed.

"Did you get our other letter?" Patrice asked. "The heavy one?"

"Not yet," I said. "But I'm sure it's on its way. The mail is very slow where I am."

"My turn," Paula said. "Mommy gave your black diary to Mr. Vincent."

"I hope he likes it," I said.

"He's funny," Paula said.

"Okay, that's it," Mom said.

"But I didn't ask a question," Paula complained.

"We had a deal. Both of you go back to the kitchen."

There was some grumbling and whining, but the two Peas obeyed.

"What time is it there?"

"A little after eight in the morning."

I hadn't even thought about what time it was. Mom had probably been waiting all night for my call.

"How's Rolf?"

"He's out of town on a business trip. He'll be back tonight. And he's going to be upset that he missed your call."

Mom sighed. "Peak, I gave it my best shot to try to talk you out of trying for the summit. But now that the decision has been made, you need to focus on the task. You can't think about me, Paula, Patrice, Rolf, or anyone else. To stay alive you are going to have to think only about yourself.

"Do you know why I quit climbing?"

"Yeah," I said. "You fell from the wall in back of—"

"No," she interrupted. "I quit because of you."

"What?"

"With some work I could have gotten my climbing condition back. In fact, the reason I went for that climb the day I fell was because Josh wanted me to get back on the circuit with him. Just before I fell I was thinking about what would happen if a rattlesnake slithered up to my baby strapped in his car seat down below. If I'd been thinking about the climb I would have realized the rock I grabbed was loose before I put weight on it. To climb at Josh's level you have to be completely selfish, Peak. When you were born I couldn't do that anymore.

"I have no doubt you have the physical ability to summit Everest or any other mountain you want. But you may not have the ability to not care. For the next few weeks you have to harden yourself inside. Your guts and heart need to be stone cold.

"I didn't do a lot of high altitude when I was climbing, but I did enough to know that the thin air messes with your brain. You need to forget everything else and concentrate on the climb. You have enough experience to know when it's over. And when it's over don't take another step higher. If you do, it could be over for good. Turn around. There's no shame in it. Live to climb another day. And when you come back down I hope that good and caring heart of yours thaws. It's the most important muscle you have. I love you, Peak."

And with this she cut the connection. I don't know how long I lay there thinking about what she said, but I can tell you there were plenty of tears. As the blue light through the tent faded to dark I was still lying there when the flap opened.

It was Josh. "You have the sat phone?"

I sat up. "Yeah . . . sorry. I should have brought it back." I gave it to him.

"So, you talked to your mom?"

"Yes."

"One thing we need to get straight," he said. "Getting Sun-jo to the top is not a backup plan. I'm giving him a shot because I owe him and Zopa."

"What do you mean?"

"Two years ago Ki-tar saved my life."

"Sun-jo's father?"

"Up on K2."

"You're the climber who survived."

"We'd been snowed in for three days. No food, no Os, no hope of survival. I watched my climbing party die one by one until I was the only one left. I should have been next, but Ki-tar came up the mountain through the worst blizzard I've ever seen. He came alone. None of the other Sherpas would come with him. He all but carried me back down. When we got to Base we stumbled into the Aid tent. I took one cot; Kitar took the other. While Leah was treating my frostbite and giving me IV fluids, the man who saved my life died not four feet away from me. His heart gave out. I didn't even get a chance to thank him. I thought you ought to know."

He closed the flap and I heard his footsteps crunching through the snow as he walked away.

UNREST

BEING SELFISH AND FOCUSED turned out not to be a problem.

After Josh dropped the K2 bomb in my tent, he dropped a second bomb on his clients. He told them about his plan to get me to the summit. I wasn't invited to the meeting, but I certainly experienced the aftermath of the explosion the next morning.

I slept late and woke up sore and famished. It had snowed a couple of feet during the night and I had to dig my way out of the tent. When I finally got to my feet and looked around I was surprised how much the camp had emptied out. (I guess I was so upset the day before I hadn't noticed.) Most of the big commercial operations were still in place, but it looked like at least a third of the smaller expeditions had pulled up stakes.

I glanced up at Captain Shek's compound and was tempted to give him a wave, but decided not to. I didn't have time for juvenile antics. I had to stay focused and disciplined if I wanted to get to the summit. Besides, I was starving and the delicious white smoke billowing from the mess tent's chimney was calling to me. Inside was food, warmth, and conversation, but I was a little worried about the conversation part. I didn't want to get too close to anyone and catch the bug that was threatening everyone's climb.

I needn't have worried about the conversation part because as soon as I stepped inside all conversation ceased. The only sound was the hiss of the gas burner and the clatter of the lid on the boiling noodle pot. There were ten people inside the tent and they were all staring at me. None of them were smiling. I would have turned around and left if I wasn't so hungry.

"Speak of the devil," the cowboy from Abilene drawled. He looked like he had lost twenty pounds since the last time I saw him. In fact, all the climbers looked like they had dropped weight. None of them were eating.

"What's going on?" I said as casually as I could with ten pairs of eyes glaring at me. I walked to the shelf and grabbed a plate.

"We're having a meeting," someone said.

"A private meeting," someone else said.

That was obvious. There wasn't a single person from HQ there. No cook. No film crew. No Sherpas.

"I'm just getting something to eat," I said. "It'll only take a minute and I'll get out of your way."

"Well," the cowboy said, "while we got you here maybe you can fill us in on when you found out your daddy was planning to put you on the top of the mountain."

What goes around comes around. Now I knew how Sunjo must have felt the week before. I scooped a pile of noodles onto my plate, but my appetite was quickly going away.

"Not until I got over here," I hedged, then put a forkful of noodles into my mouth, hoping I wouldn't have to answer any more questions on my way out the door with my plate.

"Course you realize the noodles you're eating, the plate

they're on, and maybe even the parka you're wearing were paid for by the people sitting in this mess tent."

This was an exaggeration, but he had a point, so I set my plate on the table and walked out, hoping that one of them would call me back in and say they were kidding. No one did.

The HQ tent was less hostile, but not much cheerier. Josh, Thaddeus, Leah, and the others seemed to be having a meeting of their own.

"I was just over at the mess tent," I said.

"How was their mood?" Thaddeus asked.

"Ugly."

"They'll get over it," Josh said. "It's been a rough climbing season what with the weather and everyone getting sick. I've seen it all before. As soon as we get a couple people to the top everything will be fine."

No one else in the room seemed to share his optimism, least of all Thaddeus, who said that he thought the climbers would sue Peak Experience and would probably win.

"Did you tell them about Sun-jo?" I asked.

"No," Josh said. "That would have sent them over the edge. That's our little secret, although Shek seems to have figured it out. We're going to shift everything again. Zopa, Sun-jo, Yogi, and Yash are the C team. They're still on our climbing permit, but they're on their own. Peak, you're on the A team with me. We'll divide the film crew between the teams. As soon as JR is better we'll start him filming the A and B teams. We probably won't use any of the footage, but the fact they're being interviewed for the documentary might improve their attitudes." He looked at Leah. "What's your best guess about when this virus will run its course?"

"A week, maybe longer." She looked like she was suffering from it, too. "The bigger problem is the aftereffects. Because we can't exercise and can't keep food down we're losing our conditioning. Even under ideal circumstances it will be difficult for any of us to summit."

"There's nothing we can do about that," Josh said. "We'll either make it or we won't. And that's no different than any other year."

The tent flap opened and the Texan stepped inside.

"Glad you're all here," he said. "We've been talking and we thought you'd like to know that none of us are climbing with the boy. We didn't spend our money, time, and effort to get a kid up to the summit." He looked at me. "It's nothing personal, son. I think you landed right in the middle of this mess just like we did."

"Thanks for telling me," Josh said. "But I decide who goes to the summit and who's on what team."

The Texan gave him a hard smile. "Well, Josh, you're the boss. But if you decide we have to climb with your boy, then we're not climbing at all. We'll head home and y'all will have to deal with our lawyers."

"Well, y'all might as well pack up and leave today," Josh said angrily. "Two or three years from now you might win your case and maybe even get some of your money back, but none of you will have made it to the top of the world."

If the Texan had had a six-shooter strapped around his waist I think he would have drawn it. Instead, he glared at Josh for a moment, then stomped out of the tent.

"He's bluffing," Josh said confidently.

Thaddeus didn't look nearly as confident, nor did anyone else.

In keeping with my mother's suggestion about being selfish I did not step forward and offer to give up my spot. I might have, if I thought Josh would refuse my selfless sacrifice for the team, but I wasn't sure what he would do. The argument we'd had from the day before was far from resolved. And nobody had mentioned it, but the delay from my team change meant that there was a good chance I wouldn't get to the summit before my fifteenth birthday. Both Josh and Thaddeus had to have figured this out. The bottom line was that if Sun-jo made it to the top they didn't need me.

THE NEXT COUPLE DAYS I kept a low profile, which wasn't hard since no one wanted anything to do with me. Josh's clients didn't pack up and leave, but they didn't back off, either. I think they were sticking around to see if Josh would back off. There were no more complaints about my eating "their" food in the mess tent, but the silent treatment and resentful glares continued.

Instead of getting enmeshed in the mountain madness I went climbing. One thing Camp Four had taught me was that I needed to hone my ice-climbing techniques. I think one of the reasons I had had such a difficult time climbing to the Col was my clumsy crampon moves. I hadn't done a lot of ice climbing. Efficiency saves energy, and energy is as elusive as air the higher you go.

I found an ice wall about a half mile outside camp and spent hours every day trying different routes to the top. I slipped, fell, and scraped myself, but I got a little better with each climb.

At night I stayed in my tent writing in my second Moleskine and tried to visualize my final assault on the summit. I even went so far as to make a special prayer flag. I took one of the yellow flags and carefully drew a mountain on it with a blue Sharpie. I hung it inside my tent, staring at it for hours. On top of the summit is a pole buried in the ice with a metal wire hanging from it with dozens of prayer flags beaten by the winds. Over and over again I imagined myself struggling up to that pole and tagging Everest.

Captain Shek was still looking for Sun-jo. Every morning when I headed to the wall he had a soldier follow me. I guess he thought my practice climbs were a ruse to meet secretly with the mystery boy. I actually didn't mind being followed. If I had an accident at least there would be someone around to help me, or run back to Base and get help.

Zopa, Yogi, and Yash were staying at Base Camp but keeping a low profile. I saw them once in a while, but we hadn't spoken since we got back. I suspected Captain Shek was watching them, too, and they were keeping their distance.

On the third day we got word that nine climbers had reached the summit from the north side—virtually every climber who tried that day. Now, you would think this news would be received with great joy, and on the surface it was, but just below the surface was a great deal of jealousy and resentment.

"If we hadn't gotten sick . . ."

"If Josh hadn't abandoned us on the trip to the mountain . . ."

"If he hadn't brought his son to Everest . . ."

"That could have been us. We could be headed home in a few days . . ."

"There may not be another window . . ."

And other complaints were whispered just loud enough for me to hear in the mess tent that evening during dinner.

The carping was interrupted by the appearance of Josh and Thaddeus along with the film crew. I hadn't seen any of them in the mess tent since I returned from Camp Four. Like the other climbers, JR, Jack, and Will had lost weight and still looked a little weak, but better than they had on the way down.

"If your health continues to improve," Josh began, "and if the weather is good, I hope to start the teams up to the summit in a week to ten days."

"Tomorrow morning we'll start filming interviews with you for the documentary," JR added.

The teams were not impressed by either announcement.

"You still planning to put your son on the top?" the Texan asked.

"Yes," Josh said. "Are you still planning to quit if I do?"

"If he goes we leave. That's the deal."

He didn't look like he was bluffing. Nor did the others. These were not professional climbers. They were all successful businesspeople and very used to getting their way.

"Suit yourselves," Josh said with a sad grin.

I had a bad feeling that Josh was the one bluffing, not them. He was going to blink first. And if he didn't, Thaddeus would blink for him.

BLINK

THE NEXT MORNING I was enduring another uncomfortable breakfast at a separate table from my team members when Josh and Thaddeus came into the tent.

I thought they were going to make an announcement about the filming schedule or something, but instead Josh said, "We've reached a decision."

He took a sheet of paper out of his pocket and slowly unfolded it. "B team, led by Pa-sang, will consist of the following members." He read off the names. "A team, which I'll lead, will be . . ." Then he read off another list of names with one very important omission.

My name.

Before I could find my voice the Texan spoke up, sounding almost as stunned as I felt. "Are you saying Peak isn't getting a summit shot?"

"Did you hear me read off his name?" Josh asked tersely.

"No," the Texan said quietly.

It's a ploy, I thought desperately. Otherwise Josh would have told me about the decision before this brutal announcement. He was trying to get their sympathy. Trying to get them to say: "Now, just hold on a minute, Josh. We didn't really mean for you to . . ." It was brilliant! If they decided I should come they couldn't grouse about it later.

I waited for those magic words, but they didn't come.

Instead Josh looked at me. "I'm sorry, Peak, I've been a jackass about this. They're right. This is their climb. They're paying the tab."

I thought he was overplaying it and hoped he knew what he was doing. I looked at the Texan. Now was the time for him to say, "Ah shucks, we were just having fun with you. Of course you can summit Everest with us . . ."

Instead he said, "Well, that's settled, then."

"Wait a second!" I said. "That's not fair. I worked just as hard as anyone here to get up to Camp Four."

"Let it go, Peak," Josh said quietly.

"I won't let it go!" I almost knocked over my chair standing up.

"You don't have a choice," Josh said, raising his voice. "It's all been arranged. Zopa's packing your gear right now. You and he and his Sherpas are heading to Kathmandu. The truck's waiting."

I stared at him in disbelief. It wasn't a ploy. He'd blinked!

"I'm sorry it didn't work out," he continued. "Maybe we can try again next year. You're young. You'll get plenty of chances to get to the summit."

"I don't believe this."

"I'll help you pack."

"Forget it!" I pushed past him and ran outside.

By the time I got to my tent, my gear was already in the truck and ready to go. So, it was all planned. Zopa, Yogi, and Yash were sitting in the bed waiting for me.

I wiped away my frozen tears. "You should have told me!"

Zopa shook his head. "Better to learn the way you did."

"The only thing I've learned is that you and my father are liars!"

"We must leave," Zopa said calmly. "We have a long way to go before dark."

I glared at him expecting more, but it was clear the discussion (if you want to call it that) was over. The driver started the truck.

As we pulled out of camp Josh stepped out of the mess tent and waved at me. I returned the wave with a gesture of my own. He returned the insult by giving me his trademark grin. If Zopa hadn't grabbed my collar I would have jumped out of the back of the truck and killed him with my bare hands.

I could not believe how quickly it had all come to an end. I mean, I knew I might not make it to the top of Everest, but I thought it would be due to weather, injury, or endurance . . . not some stupid business decision.

Josh hadn't bothered to mention what I was supposed to do once I got back to Kathmandu. Wait for him, I suppose. Or maybe I was being sent down to Chiang Mai. It didn't matter. As soon as I got to wherever I was going I would call Mom and find out if things had cooled off enough for me to go back to New York. The only thing I knew for sure was that I was not going to have anything to do with Joshua Wood ever again.

We bumped along the rough road for a couple of miles until we came to a roadblock manned by Chinese soldiers. They checked our papers, then thoroughly searched the truck. This is when I realized that Sun-jo wasn't with us. I was so mad when I got booted out of camp, I hadn't even thought about him. I had to wait to ask Zopa until we were back on the road.

"Where's Sun-jo?"

"He's waiting for us up ahead," Zopa said.

It looked like Sun-jo wasn't getting his shot at the summit, either. I guess Captain Shek had made it too risky. Shamefully, this made me feel a little better.

A couple miles later the truck slowed down. I looked over the top of the cab expecting to see Sun-jo, but it was just a yak and a porter heading up to Base Camp. When we drew up next to them the driver stopped. The porter was Gulu. He gave me a toothless smile, then he and Zopa talked for a while, but I couldn't understand what they were saying. When they finished, Gulu waved, then continued toward Base Camp.

We drove down the road for another mile or so, then came to another stop. At this rate it would take us a year to get to Kathmandu. Yogi and Yash hopped out of the truck and started unloading gear.

"What's going on?"

"Team C," Zopa answered.

"What are you talking about?"

Instead of answering Zopa pulled a crumpled piece of paper out of his pocket and handed it to me.

Sorry about the dramatics, but we had to make it look good so Captain Shek would think you and Sun-jo were gone and stop looking for him. I also had to appease my bonehead clients. It was the only way I could get you to the summit before your birthday. Zopa's idea. (I told you he was cagey.) He'll take you up to ABC along a different route. He's under strict orders to keep you alive. If he doesn't, your mom will kill me. I hope you make it to the top, but if you don't, no worries.

Josh

I read the note over twice, then looked up at Zopa. He was smiling.

"We will take a shortcut to ABC," he said. "But we will have to move quickly before Captain Shek discovers our deceit."

I wasn't sure if I was angry or happy with him and Josh. It had been a cruel trick. I understood why they had done it, but they should have trusted me to play a role. I could have pulled it off, and I was about to tell Zopa this when Sun-jo came over the top of a small hill and waved.

Aside from the rumbled porter clothes and the grass in his hair from Gulu's yak, he looked ready to climb.

SHORTCUT

GULU HAD HAULED a lot more than Sun-jo out of the porter camp. On the other side of the hill was a small mountain of climbing gear. Coils of rope, oxygen bottles, masks, tents, food . . . I wondered how we were going to get it to the upper camps.

On our backs, as it turned out, because Zopa went right to work dividing the gear into five separate piles. As he sorted through the stuff I asked Sun-jo what was going on. He didn't know much more than I did. He said that Gulu had woken him in the middle of the night and told him that they had to leave the porter camp right away.

"At first I thought Captain Shek had discovered I was there," he said. "But when we were safely out of camp, Gulu told me that Zopa was leading you and me to the summit in a separate expedition from your father's, but still on his permit."

I didn't tell him about how I found out because I was still mad about it, and a little embarrassed.

Yogi and Yash's loads were bigger than ours, but Sun-jo and I still had plenty to carry. We had most of the food divided between us. Zopa laughed as we grunted under the extra weight. "It will become lighter as you eat your way through the contents," he said.

THERE IS A REASON WHY Base Camp and all the other camps above it are situated where they are. The traditional route may not be the shortest way up the mountain, but it is the safest and easiest. (Not that anything is safe or easy on Everest.) Zopa's "shortcut" might have been shorter, but it was ten times more difficult than the regular route. Our first obstacle was a vast field of jagged ice sticking out of the ground like great white shark teeth. Sun-jo and I used our walking poles so we didn't slip and impale ourselves. The Sherpa brothers didn't bother with the poles, forging ahead like they were ice-skating until they were two tiny dots on the horizon. I think Zopa could have easily kept up with them, but he slowed his pace, staying about a hundred yards ahead of us so he could glance back once in a while and make sure we hadn't stumbled and were bleeding out on the frozen fangs.

By the time we caught up to them late that afternoon, Yogi and Yash had the camp set up, food on the stove, and were amusing themselves by throwing their ice axes at a wall of ice that appeared to brush the sky.

My legs were shaking uncontrollably from fatigue. My neck and shoulders felt like they had been worked over by a sledgehammer. My only consolation was that Sun-jo looked more done-in than me. He didn't even have the strength to get the pack off his back. It took us two hot mugs of tea before we could talk.

By the third mug of tea I was able to focus enough to take a good look at the wall. It seemed to run for miles in both directions. I figured the next morning we would follow it until we came to a pass then make our way to the top.

When I mentioned this to Zopa he laughed and pointed directly above us. "This is the pass," he said.

"You're kidding."

He shook his head.

There wasn't a single handhold or foothold for as far as I could see. It made the ice wall I'd been practicing on look like an indoor rock climbing wall.

After dinner Zopa turned on the radio and we listened to the mountain chatter. Three more people had made it to the summit that morning. Eight had turned back within a few hundred feet of the top. A climber had broken her leg up at ABC. The virus seemed to have run its course, and everyone who had stuck it out at Base Camp was rapidly getting better.

I was about ready to call it a day and crawl into my tent when Josh came on the radio making small talk with one of the other expedition leaders up at Camp Four. This was very unusual. Josh was a firm believer that the radio should only be used to transmit important information. He hated it when people used it like a cell phone.

They talked about the weather, the woman with the broken leg, and scheduling summit attempts.

"Heard you had a falling-out with your son," the leader said.

There were no secrets on the mountain.

"Yeah, he left," Josh said. "But we'll patch it up when I get down. He's a good kid. I think Captain Shek was going to try to yank his climbing permit, anyway. Not that I would have let him."

"Is Shek still hunting for that other kid?"

"Yep. Still on the warpath. He detained a porter this afternoon named Gulu. He let him go after a pretty tough grilling, but Gulu didn't know anything. That kid left here weeks ago. Not sure what he's trying to prove. I heard he was having some more soldiers trucked in. Some of them are climbers. He's going to send them up the mountain to check the higher camps. It's insane. I sent an e-mail to the Chinese government and I have my lawyers checking into other official actions. The Chinese make a lot of money on these permits. Be a shame if one overzealous soldier dried up that revenue source, but what are you going to do? Anyway, good luck at Camp Five. I'll check in with you tomorrow. Out."

Zopa switched off the radio. The entire conversation had been set up for us—at least on Josh's end. We couldn't participate, but we could learn a great deal by listening. None of us liked the idea of the Chinese climbers coming in.

"They won't be able to get past ABC," I said. "They haven't had time to acclimate."

"Perhaps," Zopa said.

"How do we get by them on the way back down?" Sun-jo asked.

Zopa shrugged. But this time I think he really meant it. He didn't know.

BY THE TIME ZOPA kicked Sun-jo and me out of our sleeping bags, Yogi and Yash were already fifty feet up the wall setting ice screws so we'd have something to hook on to. The sun was barely up. They had to have started when it was still dark. We ate quickly, packed, then strapped on our crampons and harnesses. Zopa said he was staying below to tie the packs and would climb last.

A bitter wind blasted the wall head-on, which was good because it pushed us into it. If the wind had been coming from an angle it would have blown us right off the wall.

Ice ax in each hand... Dig crampon in. Bury ax. Ice splinters in your face. Pull. Dig other crampon in. Bury ax... About sixty-five feet up I clipped onto an ice anchor and took a breather. Yogi and Yash had already reached the top, dropped ropes, and hauled up all the gear.

Zopa had just started up the wall. Sun-jo was clawing his way up twenty feet below me. He seemed to be struggling, which wasn't too surprising considering he had been sick and for the last few days, cooped up in a porter's tent. I waited until he looked up and gave him a wave. He returned it with a grim nod.

I started again, and had gotten up about three steps when I heard the yell. It took me a second to get myself anchored so I could look down. What I saw wasn't pretty. Sun-jo had slipped down about ten feet and was hanging on the edge of a protrusion by one ax. I'd seen the protrusion on the way up and knew it was too far from the wall for him to get his crampons planted in the ice.

"I'm coming!" Zopa shouted up at him, but it would take him at least forty-five minutes to reach him.

Sun-jo wouldn't be able to hold on for more than a few minutes. I was a lot closer, but the only thing harder and slower than climbing up an ice wall is climbing down an ice wall. I looked up, hoping to see Yogi or Yash, but there was no sign of them. They must have already forged ahead to set up the next camp.

I didn't even have time to think about what I was going to do next, which was just as well. I started scrambling sideways across the wall toward the gear rope, thirty feet away. Zopa continued to shout encouragement to Sun-jo. He was climbing the wall as fast as he could, but he had to know that no matter how fast he went, it wouldn't be fast enough to save his grandson.

When I finally reached the rope I gave it a tug. It seemed solid enough, but I didn't know if it would hold my weight. The brothers might not have anchored it properly because they were just hauling gear with it.

"I'm slipping," Sun-jo said desperately.

"I'll be there in a minute!" I shouted.

"Hang on, Sun-jo!" Zopa shouted, catching on to what I was trying to do. "Don't give up!"

I wanted to test the rope more but there wasn't time. I hooked on to it and gave it all my weight. It stretched a little, but held. I swallowed my heart and crabbed my way back toward Sun-jo. When I got directly above him I quickly hooked the rope to an ice screw I knew was secure and rappelled to him, getting the rope hooked on his harness just as his ax slipped from the ice.

"Got him!" I shouted down to Zopa, then looked at Sun-jo. "You okay?"

He nodded.

He was crying.

So was I. Apparently I had forgiven him.

IT TOOK US another hour to get to the top. Zopa got there about ten minutes after us, looking concerned and relieved.

"Nothing broken?" he asked.

Sun-jo shook his head.

"What happened?"

"My ax broke."

Zopa nodded, then looked at me. "Thank you."

"You can thank Yogi and Yash for securing that rope," I said. The first thing I did when we got to the top was check it. The rope was tied to a carabiner attached to a three-inch ice bolt that wasn't going anywhere. Sun-jo and I could have played Tarzan on that rope all day long.

"But you didn't know that," Zopa said.

"Yeah . . . well," I said, a little embarrassed, "Yogi and Yash know what they're doing."

"Not always," Zopa said. "One of the axes Sun-jo was using today was the same one they were throwing at the wall yesterday afternoon."

Uh-oh. I suspected they were going to hear about that when we caught up to them—and I was right. When we got to camp, Zopa took Yogi and Yash to the side and spoke to them for a good ten minutes. He never raised his voice, but when they came back they looked like he had whipped them.

"TWO TRUCKLOADS of Chinese soldiers got here today . . ." Josh was talking to a different expedition leader who had just arrived at ABC. ". . . along with six military climbers. The place looks like an army encampment."

"Glad I'm up here," the leader said.

"Well, you're not off the hook. From what I hear they're heading up the mountain tomorrow morning to check everybody's papers. If you don't have your passport, visa, and permit they're going to boot you off the mountain."

"We have them. What's his problem?"

"When the truck that Zopa and my son left on yesterday got to the second checkpoint, Zopa and my son weren't on it. The driver claimed they got on a second truck and went another way."

“I hope your son’s okay.”

“No worries. Zopa wouldn’t let anything happen to him. I’m sure they’re well on their way to Nepal by now. I thought I’d just give you a heads-up about what’s going on down here.”

“Thanks,” the other leader said. “What about the Chinese climbers? Are they any good?”

“They’re gung ho and well equipped. They pulled them off a high-altitude climb, but I’m not sure where they were. I wouldn’t be surprised if they tried for the summit while they’re up there. I know I would.”

“I hear you. It’s going to get crowded at the top.”

Zopa and the brothers spread a map out and started talking in Nepalese.

“What’s going on?”

“Zopa says we can’t stay in any of the camps until we reach Camp Five,” Sun-jo explained. “They’re picking alternative sites.”

I looked at the map. We were just about parallel to Camp Two, but seven or eight miles to the north. It would take us at least another day to pull up even with ABC.

We could be up on the summit in less than a week.

CAMP 3½

ZOPA PUSHED US HARD the next two days. We were out of camp before dawn climbing with headlamps. Yogi and Yash were always long gone before we started out, and we didn't see them until we stopped at the end of the day.

I had no idea where we were, but according to my altimeter watch, we were gaining altitude. (Not that I needed the watch: Every breath was painful now.) At the end of the day it was all Sun-jo and I could do to eat a little food, drink, and then crawl into our bags.

On the third morning I was surprised to open my eyes and see sunlight coming through the blue tent fabric. I looked over at Sun-jo and saw that he was staring at the light, too.

We had barely talked the past few days. No time, no breath.

"How are you doing?" I asked.

"Not well," Sun-jo said.

"You've done okay the last couple of days."

He shook his head. "It has been very hard."

That was an understatement. We had done several technical climbs the past forty-eight hours. It had been some of the most difficult climbing I had ever done.

"Any idea where we are?"

Sun-jo sat up with a groan. "Feels like we're on the summit."

I laughed, which turned into a short but painful coughing fit. When I recovered I said, "Maybe Zopa is going to give us a day off."

"Not likely."

We went through the contortions of getting dressed in our small tent, then crawled out. Light snow and freezing fog. We hadn't seen the sky in three days. Yogi and Yash were crouching next to the camp stove.

Yogi said something that made Sun-jo blanch.

"What?" I asked.

"Zopa is sick."

I understood why he was upset. Zopa didn't get sick. Zopa was the iron man. He had seemed fine the night before when we got to camp. We hurried over to his tent. He looked terrible—bloodshot eyes, runny nose, pale—but he managed to sit up in his sleeping bag when he saw us.

"We will go up to Camp Four this afternoon," he said.

He wasn't going anywhere in his condition.

"The virus?" I asked.

"I think so," he answered with a slight smile. "Or maybe it's just age."

"Regardless," Sun-jo said, "we should go back down. We need to get you help."

"We cannot go down," Zopa said. "The Chinese are waiting for us. Our only escape is up."

"We have to come down eventually," I said.

"But not on this side."

"What are you talking about?"

"Nepal is a little more than a mile away from here."

I thought he was delirious or something. It would take us days to reach the Friendship Bridge into Nepal.

He took out the map and pointed to the south side of the summit. "This is Nepal," he said. He pointed to the north side. "This is Tibet." He walked his fingers up the north side of Everest, then down the south side.

"You mean we're not coming back down the north side into Tibet?" I asked.

"When you reach the summit," he said, "you will head south into Nepal."

"But we're not set up for the south side," I protested. "We don't have tents or gear or—"

"Sherpas will help you," Zopa said. "Friends of mine. We have already gotten word to them. They will be waiting on the other side. Yogi and Yash will take you to the summit."

"What about you?" Sun-jo asked.

"As you can see I am in no condition to climb. Camp Four is as far as I will be going."

"Then we'll wait until you get better," Sun-jo insisted.

"That's right," I said. "I don't care if I get up to the summit by my birthday. It's not important—to me, anyway. We'll set up a camp somewhere, or stay right here until you get better."

Zopa shook his head. "We don't have enough food or supplies."

"Yogi and Yash can get more supplies from the other Sherpas."

"That is not the only obstacle," Zopa said. "The weather. In three days it will be good for a summit attempt. You will have to be in position."

I glanced back outside. It was snowing harder and the fog had thickened. "How can you know that?"

Zopa shrugged.

He was impossible! "Okay," I said, "so the weather breaks and we make it to the summit and somehow make it down the south side. How are *you* going to get past the Chinese soldiers on the north side?"

"I'm a Nepalese citizen in Tibet with legal papers. Captain Shek has no grounds to arrest me. You saw what happened the last time he tried. I don't think I will be caught, but if I am, the very worst he can do is deport me, which is what I want, anyway. I'll see both of you on the other side."

"I don't think I can make it to the summit," Sun-jo said. "I had a lot of trouble yesterday."

"I'm afraid I've put you in a terrible situation, Sun-jo," Zopa said. "You will have to make it to the summit now."

I thought about offering to stay with Zopa at Camp Four and help him down the mountain after he got better. But this was clearly not in keeping with my mother's instructions to stay selfish. And I *did* want to get to the summit. The debate was resolved by Zopa.

He gave me a monkish smile. "I don't need your help, Peak. But Sun-jo will."

I just stared at him, relieved I didn't have to make the decision and stunned that he seemed to have read my mind. "How—"

Zopa held up his hand. "Sun-jo will not reach the summit without your help," he said. "I need to rest. And so do both of you. We have a hard climb ahead of us."

SUN-JO TOOK ZOPA'S ADVICE. I tried to sleep but couldn't. I joined Yogi and Yash at the fire. Yogi pulled out an oxygen tank and mask out of his pack. He showed me how to attach the mask to the regulator, then he held up two fingers, indicating I was to set the dial to two liters per minute. Then, using Yash as a model, he showed me how to put on the mask.

When he finished he took everything apart and had me put it all back together. It wasn't as easy as it looked. I had to pull off my outer mitts, and my fingers went numb in spite of the fact that I was still wearing gloves. This reminded me that I still had JR's little video camera in my pack. I had completely forgotten about it. I needed to start filming our trip. (Which should give you a little idea of how the brain functions, or doesn't function, at high altitudes.)

I managed to get the mask hooked up to the tank, then I put the mask on and tried to adjust the straps for a tight fit over my nose and mouth. The mask was cold, uncomfortable, and a little claustrophobic. Yash had a perfect solution to the discomfort. He turned on the oxygen.

In my entire life I had never felt anything so wonderful. The Os flowed into my body like some kind of magic elixir. For the first time in weeks I felt warm, sharp, and strong. The feeling was short-lived because Yogi turned it off almost immediately. Reluctantly, I took off the mask. The Sherpa brothers were smiling at me. Yogi said something in Nepalese, then held up five fingers.

"Got it," I said. "Not until Camp Five."

Theoretically, you could use Os all the way up the mountain. The problem was you would have to use a half dozen Sherpas to carry enough oxygen tanks to get up the mountain. The tanks didn't last that long.

Yogi and Yash left around noon. A couple of hours later

Zopa came out of his tent looking like a corpse emerging from a tomb. Three mugs of hot tea seemed to revive him . . . a little. I packed his gear, then roused Sun-jo, who looked a lot better after his nap.

We started out for Camp Four. This time Sun-jo and I had to wait for Zopa. About halfway there, he put on an oxygen mask and cranked it up. This certainly put a little more spring in his step. I was envious.

CAMPS FIVE AND SIX

BECAUSE OF OUR LATE START, I thought Camp Four was close, but we didn't get to the dreaded wall leading up to it until well after dark.

"We're climbing the wall at night?" I asked, shocked.

Zopa took off his mask. "It's the only way to get into Camp Four unnoticed. Everyone will be asleep."

They would be in their tents all right—the wind was howling and it hadn't stopped snowing all day. But from our last experience I knew they wouldn't be sleeping. If they were like me when I was up there, they would be lying in their sleeping bags wondering if there was enough air to keep them alive through the night.

The last time we were here it took me over five hours to reach the top and I nearly gave up on the way. The weather was worse now—and it was dark.

Yogi and Yash had thrown a rope over the side for us to use.

"You'll need headlamps," Zopa said.

"Right," I said.

Slide the jumar up the rope, step, breathe, jumar, step, jumar, think, look up, think again, step, rest, rest, rest, hug the wall, pray... The same routine. But in a strange way the climb was easier, or at least less scary, with the headlamp. The light kept me focused on the ice and rock in front of me. I had no idea where the top or bottom was until a light appeared over the edge about ten feet above me. It was Yogi, although it was hard to tell, bundled up like he was. I managed to get to the top without his having to grab me. As I rested on my knees trying to catch my breath and not puke, I looked at my watch. I had climbed the wall in less than five hours this time.

Fifteen minutes later Sun-jo came over the top, looking like he was about to pass out. I shouted in his ear that he had made it up the wall a half hour faster than he had the last time. This seemed to cheer him up. He managed to get to his feet.

Zopa was last. He was in terrible shape. It took all three of us to pull him over the edge, and when we got him there he didn't move. I checked his oxygen tank. It was empty. Yogi hurried off and came back with a fresh tank and Yash. They got the Os flowing and carried Zopa to their tent. After an hour or so he recovered enough to open his eyes and drink something. A few minutes later he asked the brothers if they had heard anything from Josh.

The Chinese soldier climbers had reached ABC that afternoon and were planning on staying there a day or two before climbing to Camp Four. They had checked everyone's papers and searched all the tents. The climbers at ABC said the soldiers were in great shape and had made terrific time. There was no doubt they were going to try for the summit.

This seemed like the worst possible news, but Zopa didn't seem at all disturbed by it.

"You will be a day ahead of them. Tonight and tomorrow you will rest. The following morning, before light, you'll climb to Camp Five."

"What about you?" Sun-jo asked.

"Do you really think they are going to be worried about a sick old monk when they get up here? If they really are such good climbers, the soldiers will all want to try for the summit. Which of them will stay behind to escort the old man down the mountain?" He gave a wheezy laugh. "By the time they get back here I will be gone."

"Why can't we just go up to Camp Five when it gets light?" I asked. "We'll be just that much farther ahead of the soldiers."

"There will be a storm in a few hours," Zopa answered. "Tomorrow morning is your window."

THE STORM HIT US MIDMORNING. If we had left when I wanted we would have been about halfway to Camp Five. And we would have died, along with the three climbers who *did* leave that morning. None of them made it to Camp Five, and nobody could help them. The weather was too severe.

I tried to write in my Moleskine and found that I couldn't concentrate long enough to string more than two or three words together at a time. After a while I gave up and managed to get a little sleep, and so did Sun-jo, mostly because there was nothing else to do but lie in the tent. Zopa didn't want us wandering around camp (not that we had the energy), and the storm was so bad, everyone there was hunkered down waiting for it to stop.

About eight o'clock that night it did, suddenly. One moment the wind and snow were threatening to blow our tent away; the next moment it was perfectly calm. I stuck my head outside the tent, along with everyone else in camp, and saw a perfectly clear sky overhead scattered with bright stars.

Yash left for Camp Five three hours ahead of us to get the

camp ready. Yogi stuck his head into our tent an hour before we were to leave and told us to pack our gear. We weren't taking much with us. Most of what we needed would be waiting for us at Camp Five. Yogi and Yash had hauled it up the last time we were at Camp Four.

Before we took off we checked in with Zopa. He was sitting up drinking a mug of tea. He was off the Os and some of the color had returned to his face, but he still looked pretty weak.

"Speed is everything now. If you stay in the death zone too long you will die. If you don't reach the summit by one thirty-five P.M. the day you leave Camp Six, I have asked Yogi and Yash to turn you around. It is better to get caught by the Chinese than it is to die on the mountain."

This seemed to contradict his plan to get Sun-jo over the top to safety, but he was right. From Camp Six you have to reach the summit and return in about eighteen hours. Oxygen or not, there was a limit to how long you could survive above Camp Six. If we made the summit we would have to reach the top camp on the other side in eighteen hours.

"Have Yogi and Yash been to the summit?" I asked. It had been a question on my mind since Zopa had announced he wasn't taking us there himself.

"Of course," Zopa said. "Three times."

"Good," I said. "Does Josh know you're not coming with us?"

Zopa shook his head, then gave us a blessing and said, "I'll see you both in Kathmandu. Now go."

It was clear and bitterly cold as we left the dark camp and started up the north ridge to the summit. It was hard to keep my excitement in check. A night at Camp Five, a night at Camp Six, then the top of the world.

IT WAS MORE OF A FORCED MARCH to Camp Five than a climb. We hooked on to a series of fixed ropes. Yogi set the pace. I tried a regime of twelve steps, a minute of gasping to recover, then another twelve steps. After an hour it was down to about eight steps, and I'm not sure how many minutes to recover. It was hard to believe that some climbers had made it to the summit without any supplemental Os at all. Josh was one of them, although I suspected on this trip he would be sucking down the Os, if for no other reason than to stay sharp so he didn't lose one of his clients.

The sun came up and gave us the best view of Everest's pyramidal summit yet. It was enormous. Coming off the top was a disk of ice crystals against the blue sky. The sight inspired my sluggish brain to remember the camera, which I had put in my pocket before we left Camp Four. I shouted ahead at Sun-jo to wait up, which he was more than happy to do. When I got to him I took off my outer mittens, pushed the record button, and tried to imitate JR as best as I could.

"What are you feeling right now?" I asked. "You're less than a mile from the highest point on earth." I had him framed perfectly against the summit.

"Frightened," Sun-jo said. "And hopeful. And worried about my grandfather. I had no idea it would be this hard."

That's about all my unmittened fingers could take.

"I can film you now if you like," Sun-jo offered.

"Nah, that's all right. We have to get moving."

About half an hour later we saw our first corpse. Sun-jo

saw it first. I walked up to him as he was staring down at it. Yogi had breezed by as if he hadn't noticed but I bet he had. It was a woman. About fifty feet away was another corpse but I couldn't tell what it was because it was lying facedown.

I had never seen a dead person, let alone a frozen dead person. She looked more like a wax figure than a former human being, and in a way this was even more disturbing to me. She had been there a while if her shredded clothes were any indication. It looked like she had died sitting up and had fallen over on her side. She was only a few hours from her tent at Camp Four. I'm not sure how long we stood there staring, and we would have stood there a lot longer if Yogi hadn't shouted at us to hurry up. After five more corpses I stopped looking.

At noon we came to a steeper part of the north ridge. It was much colder. The fixed ropes were frozen and Sherpas had chipped shallow steps into the ice to make it easier to climb.

Yogi waited for us to catch up to him. He pointed to the tents down at Camp Four, then up to tents at Camp Five and said something in Nepalese.

"Halfway," Sun-jo translated. "Six hours to go."

To make that six hours worse, the wind picked up. We had to bend over as we climbed so we weren't blown off the ridge. My initial excitement was long gone. I think the only thing that kept me going were the Os waiting for me up ahead. I don't know what kept Sun-jo going. Probably the Chinese climbers behind him and freedom ahead.

We got to Camp Five a little before seven: 25,196 feet. It seemed impossible that we could ever go any farther. It was the end of the world. And it really wasn't a camp. It was a series of cleared platforms stretching up the north ridge for at least a quarter of a mile, with absolutely no shelter from the howling wind. The big platforms could hold five or six tents, the small platforms one or two. Several of the platforms had tents on them, but it was hard to say how many people were up there. I suspected most of the tents were waiting for climbers coming up from Camp Four, or down from Camp Six after their summit attempt.

Our tiny rubble pile was just big enough for two tents pitched on the garbage of the former occupants. Yash had water boiling for tea, but what I was interested in was the mask strapped to his face pumping Os into his lungs. He was moving twice as fast as we were.

I grabbed a tank from the pile, pulled the mask out of my pack, hooked it up, and stuck my face in it. The feeling I had with the first lungful of oxygen is indescribable. *Bliss* is about as close as I can come, but it was way beyond that.

Yash helped Sun-jo set up his rig, and when he got it on we looked at each other and started laughing.

We were going to live. We might even make it to the summit.

"THE CHINESE ARE HEADING UP to Camp Four tomorrow," one of the climbers from ABC told Josh.

"You're kidding!" Josh said. "What about acclimatization?"

"These guys are acclimated. One of our climbers speaks a little Chinese. They told her they were up on K2 when they were ordered to come here. They haven't said it, but I don't think they're coming back down until they take a shot at the summit. They're like climbing machines. When are you heading up?"

"The day after tomorrow if the weather's good," Josh answered. "I was going to hold off a little longer, but I took my people out for a climb today and they all did pretty well. The virus seems to have run its course."

"We're heading up to Camp Four in the morning. We'll see you on the way back down."

"Good luck."

"Out."

This was probably the last transmission we would hear. I wondered if Josh would be worried when he didn't pass me on his way up.

I asked Sun-jo how he was doing.

"The oxygen helps, but I'm still concerned. I had a lot of trouble today."

"You're not the only one. It's hard up here."

"I have to make it," he said. "For my sisters and my mother."

Those were great reasons to risk your life, I thought. But why was *I* doing it? For Josh's business? For my ego?

Now that my brain had oxygen I found myself really missing the two Peas, my mom, and even Rolf. This got me to thinking about the corpses we saw on the way up here. Who had they left behind? These were very uncomfortable questions to fall asleep on.

THE OXYGEN WAS WONDERFUL, but the masks were a pain in the butt to sleep in. It was hard to find a position where the straps didn't dig into your face. Also, the exhaust system stank. Small pools of icy slime collected in the mouthpiece valve. When I moved my head slushy spit ran down my neck. Because of this, Sun-jo and I were up early.

We checked and rechecked our gear. Leaving something behind like a spare headlamp battery or a glove could be a death sentence.

Yogi took the lead this time, leaving Yash to take us up to Camp Six. Our first obstacle was a steep snowfield that we had to four-point with ice axes and crampons. Stupidly, I assumed that now that we were on Os, it would be like climbing at sea level. Nothing could be further from the truth.

By the time we reached the top of the snowfield my lungs were screaming for air. I thought there was something the matter with my mask or the tank had run out of oxygen, but everything was working perfectly. The two liters of oxygen didn't simulate sea level; it simply allowed me to stay alive above 25,000 feet. And there was a huge difference between lying in a tent doing virtually nothing and climbing a steep snowfield on all fours. I took the little camera out and filmed Sun-jo crabbing his way up to me. By the expression on his face I could see he was having the same O revelation I'd just had.

"I don't think I can make it." He gasped. "I'm serious, Peak; this is too much."

"We just pushed it too hard going up the field," I said with a confidence I didn't feel. "We'll just have to pace ourselves."

He nodded, but there was fear in his eyes. I knew exactly how he felt. We had passed another three or four corpses on the way up.

A few hours later I stopped to rest and looked at my altimeter watch. We had just passed 26,000 feet and were officially in the death zone. Every minute from now on we were dying a little.

We stumbled into Camp Six like three zombies. Yogi had the tents set up, but he didn't look much better than we did. He told Sun-jo to get our stove going to boil snow and drink as much water as we could. The very idea of drinking or eating anything made my stomach lurch.

I turned on the video camera and shot Sun-jo lighting the stove, or trying to light the stove. It must have taken him fifty strokes to get the cigarette lighter going in the thin air. When it finally ignited his thumb was bleeding like he had sliced it open with a knife.

We gagged down as much water and food as we could, then wrapped up in our sleeping bags to wait. Sleep was out of the question.

The inside of the tent was filled with a thin layer of frost from our breath. Every time one of us moved, the freezing crystals fell on our faces.

They say that when you die your life flashes before your eyes. Mine was passing before my eyes in slow motion like a horror movie. I think it was the corpses that did it. I thought of Mom falling off that wall, the boy I'd never met falling off the Flatiron Building, Sun-jo hanging by a thread on that ice wall, and Sun-jo's father saving my father then dying of heart failure. . . .

The only thing that stopped the depressing playback was the tent flap opening and the appearance of Yogi's masked face.

"We go," he said.

Well, not quite. It was more like: "We get ready to go." They made us drink more water, then told us to do our toilet, which is a lot easier said than done at thirty degrees below zero. Two hours later we were ready.

We left for the summit of Mount Everest.

I looked at my watch. It was 1:35 A.M. We had twelve hours to get there.

TOP OF THE WORLD

OUTSIDE CAMP SIX we picked our way across two snowfields. Yash led the way with Yogi sticking close to us. On the far side of the second field we started to encounter bare rock. I kept my eyes on Yash's headlamp. He was probably 150 yards ahead of us. Breathing was difficult and it was freezing out, but I started to think this might not be as bad as I thought. It was certainly no worse than what we had already been through.

Then to my utter shock, Yash's headlamp started to rise from the ground. I blinked several times, thinking it was some kind of optical illusion. It wasn't. He was climbing a steep wall.

"Yellow Band!" Yogi shouted above the howling wind. "Careful!"

We started up. Large chunks of yellowish sandstone broke off with almost every handhold, and the crampons strapped on our boots were worse than useless. They're made for ice, not rock, but there wasn't time to take them off. At Base Camp it would take three minutes to shuck the crampons. Up here in the thin air, it might take half an hour or longer. We didn't have a half hour to spare. And we would have to put them back on the next time we came across ice or snow, which takes longer than taking them off.

There were ropes, but most of them were rotten, flapping

uselessly in the wind. About an hour into the climb I grabbed one to help me over a difficult pitch and it popped loose from its anchor. I barely caught myself before I keeled over backward. I didn't touch another rope on the way up.

There were three steps leading to the summit and this had to be the first. But if that was the case, why had Yash called it the Yellow Band? *Must be the Sherpa nickname for it,* I thought.

Five hours later I found out I was wrong.

We got to the top just as the sun was coming up and there it was: the ridge. It looked like a gigantic dragon's tail with switchbacks and scales and complex rocky steps. I counted the so-called steps. One . . . two . . . crap . . . three. The Yellow Band was the Yellow Band. The first step was yet to come.

Yash and Sun-jo caught up to me a few minutes later. I taped them resting with their hands on their knees, then swung the camera around to the summit. Yash pointed to his watch and started toward the base of the first step.

Yogi was sitting on a rock waiting for us. He checked our oxygen tanks, made us drink something, then pointed up.

The first step was about sixty-five feet. It was 7:00 A.M. and minus thirty-five degrees out. Zopa was right about the weather again. There wasn't a cloud in the sky, but that could change in a matter of minutes.

The first ten feet led up a crack on the left side of the cliff. Next came a traverse across an unstable ledge, made much harder by our weakened legs. (Mine were shaking almost uncontrollably the entire traverse.) The final part of the climb was a wild scramble between two boulders.

We got to the top of the first step at 8:30 A.M.

The second step was twice as steep and twice as high as

the first. Before we attempted it, Yogi changed all of our oxygen tanks. Both Sun-jo and I nearly passed out while we waited for him to reconnect the precious Os.

There were aluminum ladders attached (kind of) to the wall of the first section. They moved and twisted under our weight and made a terrible scraping noise against the rock. Climbing the slippery rungs wasn't made any easier by wearing crampons. It was like trying to climb a ladder with ice skates. I was delighted to get off the ladders, but the final move to the top was much worse. It was a tension traverse where you could only use your arms, then swing up to the top by a bunch of old ropes tied to a sling. I wouldn't have thought it possible, but I watched Yogi do it without a hitch. Sun-jo was right behind me. He looked as sick about the move as I did.

I followed Yogi's route move for move, but when I grabbed the rope my crampon slipped and I found myself dangling by the rope like a dead fish with absolutely no momentum to get me to the top of the step. In addition to this I had gotten twisted around with my back to the wall.

I glanced over at Sun-jo and Yash. They stared back at me helplessly. There was nothing they could do. I looked up. Yogi was leaning over the ledge trying to reach the sling so he could pull me up. He wasn't even close. We hadn't brought any rope with us. The extra weight would slow us down and that could kill us.

I knew the longer I hung there the more fatigued my arms would become. If I waited too long for a solution, I wouldn't have the strength to execute it. I had to move. Now!

I flipped back around, smashing my face into the wall, then drove the front spikes of my crampons into the hard rock. One of them stuck, and putting weight on that leg, I was able to relieve the pressure on my arms. Holding as tight as I could with my left hand, I let my right hand go. I pulled off the outer mitten with my teeth and let it drop, then shook the arm out. (I had another pair of mittens in my pack.) I repeated the procedure with my left arm. I was going to need all the strength I could in my arms for the next move. And I hoped Yogi was paying close attention above because I was going to need his help.

I walked up the wall with my crampons until I was in a < position, then I basically stood up, hoping the crampons held. They did. At the last second I let go of the rope with my left hand, hoping I could stretch it high enough for Yogi to grab. He grabbed it, but he was still going to need help getting me up. He had taken off his outer mitts, too, and had me pretty solidly. I let my right hand go and flailed away blindly for a handhold. I found a crack, just big enough to dig the very tips of my sore fingers into. I pulled up with all the strength I had. If it didn't work, Yogi was going to have to let me drop. When I was as high as I thought I could go I brought my right knee up to my chest and tried to get my foot into the sling. I barely snagged it, but it was enough. All I had to do now was stand up and I would be within inches of the top.

Yogi dragged me over the edge and he and I lay there on our backs gasping for breath. He reached over and cranked my tank up to four and I did the same for him. Even with the extra oxygen it took us a good five minutes to catch our breath.

I wondered what was going through Sun-jo's mind after he saw that. Apparently, he had learned by my mistake because a few minutes later he swung up over the edge like a spider monkey. Yash was right behind him.

They let me rest for another fifteen minutes. I needed it. Yogi didn't turn my oxygen down until we were ready to leave. I needed that, too.

The third step was the easiest of the three for me, even though it came higher in the climb. Compared to what I had just been through, it was a breeze.

When we got to the top we saw another corpse. He was lying on his back with one arm splayed out and the other hand buried in the pocket of his down parka. The corpse looked pretty fresh. It might have been one of the German climbers who had died when we were at ABC. There was no sign of the other climber he had been with. I wondered if he had died on the way up to the summit, or the way down. I wondered how many people were waiting for him to come home. *No one climbs a mountain thinking they're not coming back down.* I looked away from the dead climber, trying to shut out Mom's warning.

Beyond the corpse lay the summit pyramid's ice field, then the summit ridge.

Yogi pointed at his watch, then held up two fingers. Two hours left.

We clipped on to ropes and started across the ice field. I don't know about Sun-jo, but this is when I shifted into summit fever. At this point I should have been completely spent, but instead I was totally juiced. Mom's warning disappeared into thin air. Poof! Nothing was going to stop me from getting to the top.

The snowfield became steeper, curving around into what I thought would be the summit, but instead we ran into fresh avalanche debris. Some of the chunks were as big as school buses. I swore. To come all this way only to be stopped by an avalanche? It would take us hours, if not days, to scramble over the debris.

Yogi pointed at the debris and shook his head.

No kidding, I thought, staring at the debris bitterly. He yanked on my sleeve. I thought he was telling me that we had to go back now. That it was over. I was going to shout that we had to try for Sun-jo's sake, even though I knew it was hopeless.

But Yogi wasn't trying to turn me around. He was pointing at another rock cliff flanking the final buttress. The debris-filled ice field was not the route to the summit.

Once again we had to traverse a narrow ledge along the face, clipping on to a rope that looked like it had been there for three hundred years. About a hundred and fifty feet along the ledge we ran into an outcropping that took a lot of finesse, and time, to get around. At the end of the traverse the route stepped up in a series of small ledges, which took us about twenty minutes to climb. We emerged onto the upper slope of the summit pyramid ice field past all the avalanche debris.

The wind was really blowing now. Yash led us to the shelter of an outcrop, where we rested for a few minutes before our final push. Yogi pointed at his watch again and stood. I took up the rear and recorded him, Sun-jo, and Yash heading for what I thought was the summit. It wasn't. When we reached the top of the ice field the real summit was revealed. The colorful prayer flags on the summit pole were fluttering in the wind 650 feet away.

We stopped again to rest, but I cut mine short.

"I'm pushing ahead!" I shouted above the deafening wind. "I'll film you coming up!" This wasn't exactly the truth. The real reason was that I couldn't wait to get to the top.

600 feet...

Two football fields. At nearly 29,000 feet it felt more like twenty miles.

Three steps... rest... three steps... rest... two steps... rest...

I discovered it was best to avoid looking up at the summit. Every time I peeked it appeared farther away, as if I were walking backward. Sun-jo, Yash, and Yogi were about a hundred feet behind me moving at the same snail's pace. I shot them for a couple minutes, then started out again.

100 feet...

90 feet...

I stopped and checked my Os, thinking the tank must be empty. It was half full, hissing out two liters per minute, which didn't seem nearly enough to keep me alive.

80 feet...

50 feet...

I looked at my watch. 1:09 P.M. Twenty-six minutes to turnaround time. I stopped to rest. I was standing at 29,003 feet, higher than any other mountain on earth: 32 feet to go.

It was cold and windy, but the weather was rarely better at this altitude. I could see for hundreds of miles in every direction. "Beautiful" doesn't describe the view, nor does "majestic." The closest word I could think of was "divine," but even that fell short of what it was like.

Sun-jo had made up some time. He was less than twenty feet away from me. Yogi and Yash were walking on either side of him. I wanted to turn around and finish the climb, but instead I took out the camera and recorded my team coming up. I could see now that Sun-jo was struggling and Yash and Yogi were actually helping him along. It was 1:19 by the time they reached me. Sun-jo fell down on his knees and was having difficulty breathing. I checked his oxygen tank gauge and saw they had already cranked it up to four liters per minute.

I gave him some time to rest, then squatted next to him. "You can do this, Sun-jo. It's only about thirty feet away. Look!" I pointed to the ridge pole.

He gazed up at the colorful prayer flags snapping in the wind and gave a dull nod, but he didn't move.

"After you touch the pole," I said, "it's all downhill."

Sun-jo shook his head. "I don't think I can do it."

"You have to do it! For your sisters. For yourself."

He continued to shake his head. I looked at Yogi and Yash. They were in as bad a shape as Sun-jo. Getting Sun-jo this far had nearly done them in. I looked at my watch. Twelve minutes to turnaround time. Even if we left right that second, I wasn't sure we would make the summit by 1:35.

"You go," Sun-jo said weakly. "I'll start back down."

"You can't go down the north side. The Chinese are waiting for you."

"I will get around them."

He and I both knew this wasn't true. I looked down the mountain. Two other climbing parties had topped the third step and were winding their way up the dragon's tail. They must have gotten a late start or had run into problems along the way. If the weather held they might be okay.

You can never tell who the mountain will allow and who it will not. . . . Sun-jo will not reach the summit without your help. . . .

"Let's go." I pulled Sun-jo to his feet.

We started back up and with each little step, Sun-jo seemed to gain strength.

25 feet. . .

20. . .

17 feet. . .

10 feet. . .

I stopped and stared up at the summit pole, then turned around and looked below.

"What's the matter?" Sun-jo asked.

I looked back up at the summit pole, then pulled my goggles down and looked at Sun-jo. "Do you know the date?"

He shook his head.

"May thirtieth," I said.

"So?"

"I think this is as far as I'm going."

"What are you talking about? The summit is only a few steps away. What does the date have to—"

"Tomorrow's your birthday. You have a reason to be here, Sun-jo. An important reason. Your future and your sisters' future. I don't have a reason for being here. I'm heading back down the north side."

Sun-jo stared at me like I was crazy, and maybe I was at that moment, but the decision I had made during the last few feet felt right. I didn't want to be the youngest person to summit Everest. Sun-jo's father died saving my father. Reaching the top would save Sun-jo and his sisters. With the money from the equipment endorsements he would receive they would all be able to go back to school.

"It is too much," Sun-jo said.

"It's nothing."

"Come with us down the south side into Nepal."

I shook my head. "If I climb down the south side everyone will know that I reached the summit. The only way down for me is the way I came up. But I do have a favor to ask." I took off my pack and found the Moleskine. The yellow prayer flag with the blue mountain was hidden in a pocket in the back of the journal. I took it out and handed it to him. "When you get to the top tie this on the pole."

"Of course, but—"

"You need to go."

Sun-jo put his thick gloves together in the Buddhist way and bowed. "Thank you, Peak. I will not forget this."

"We're running out of time. I'll tape you getting to the top so there's a record of the climb."

Sun-jo quickly explained what I was doing to Yogi and Yash. At first they looked shocked, then they both broke into broad smiles and clapped me on the back.

"Yogi is coming with you," Sun-jo said.

"I'll be all right."

"He insists," Sun-jo said, "and so do I."

"Fine."

We all shook hands and hugged, then I recorded Sun-jo and Yash taking those last ten steps. When they reached the summit of the highest mountain in the world they took off their masks and smiled and waved for the camera.

Sun-jo tied my yellow flag to the pole, then he and Yash crossed into Nepal.

DOWN THE MOUNTAINSIDE

I DON'T REMEMBER MUCH about the trip back to Camp Six. We stumbled into camp well after dark. I vaguely remember Yogi hooking up a fresh oxygen tank to my mask, but after that it's a blank. I didn't have any trouble sleeping. I know that. And I didn't have any regrets about not reaching the summit.

I woke up with spit frozen all over my face and the worst headache of my life. The oxygen tank was empty. I grabbed another one and cranked it up to six for a few minutes. That got rid of most of the headache.

Yogi and I were eager to get down and check on Zopa. We bypassed Camp Five and went directly to Camp Four. As soon as we stepped into camp we were confronted by one of the Chinese soldiers. He was dressed like a climber, except for the pistol strapped around his waist. In pretty good English he asked who we were and what we were doing.

"My name is Peak Marcello and this is Yogi Sherpa," I said. "We took supplies up to Camp Five and we're headed back down to Base Camp."

He called Captain Shek on the radio and they had a long conversation in Chinese.

"The captain wants to talk to you," the soldier said and handed me the radio.

"This is Peak Marcello," I said.

"Joshua Wood's son?"

"Right."

"What you doing on mountain?"

"Like I told your officer, I helped take some supplies to Camp Five. Josh is taking a climbing party up tomorrow."

"But you leave mountain!"

"What are you talking about?" I asked, enjoying myself immensely. "I'm up at Camp Four."

"You have big argument with you father."

"Oh that. He told me that he wasn't going to let me try for the summit. It made me mad, but at least he let me get as far as Camp Five."

"What about other boy?"

"What other boy?"

"Sun-jo!"

"Oh him," I said. "He's in Nepal." Which was the absolute truth.

"I don't believe. I have soldier bring you and Sherpa back to Base Camp."

"Whatever," I said and handed the radio back to the soldier.

They had another long conversation in Chinese, but I knew what this one was about. The other soldiers had gathered around the radio and were listening intently. The one with the radio finally signed off and shook his head with resignation.

"You don't have to escort us down," I said.

"We have orders," he said.

"That's fine with me, but we're going to Base Camp. Where else would we go?"

About that time Josh came on the radio asking for me. The soldier handed me his radio again.

"Is everything okay, Peak?"

"I guess. What's the matter with that captain?"

"I don't know. Anyway, we're headed up to ABC tomorrow, so I guess we'll see you on your way to Base Camp. Thanks for helping Yogi get those supplies up to Five."

I could see him and the others gathered at HQ monitoring the call from Captain Shek.

"No problem," I said. "Is there any way you'd reconsider giving me a shot at the summit?"

"We already talked about that, Peak. The answer is no. Maybe next year, or the year after, when you're a little older. You're not ready."

"Out." I handed the radio back, trying to look disappointed.

The soldier looked at me for a moment. "Do I have your word that you are going down to Base Camp?"

I held up my right hand. "You have my word. All I want to do right now is crawl into my tent and go to sleep."

He nodded.

Yogi and I headed over to Zopa's tent not sure what we would find. What we found was a note.

Peak,

I left Camp Four yesterday. All is well. I will see you on the road.

Zopa

I was glad to hear he was okay, but the note freaked me out. It was addressed to me! The plan had been for me to top the mountain with Sun-jo and cross into Nepal. How could Zopa possibly have known what I was planning to do?

I didn't know what I was planning to do until I was ten feet away from the summit!

YOGI AND I WOKE UP early and left Camp Four before anyone was awake. I wanted to give the soldiers an out so they could tell the captain that we had left before they were up.

When we got to ABC we were met by more soldiers. They were in uniform and looked uncomfortably cold. Once again I was given a radio with a very angry Captain Shek on the other end.

"You leave Camp Four!"

"Right."

"Without soldiers!"

"We left before light. We didn't want to wake them. Besides, we know our way down to Base Camp. We don't need an escort."

"Soldiers at ABC escort you!"

"Fine."

The two soldiers picked for the duty were delighted to be leaving ABC.

We ran into Josh and his clients just as they were arriving at Camp Two. They must have left Base Camp early, because they had made good time. Josh took me to the side out of earshot of the Chinese soldiers.

"Did you make the summit?" he asked quietly.

"No."

"What happened?"

"Ran out of steam."

"No worries," he said. "What about Zopa, Sun-jo, and Yash?"

"Zopa got sick and didn't get past Camp Four. I don't know where he is now. I was hoping that you'd seen him."

Josh shook his head. "I'm sure he's fine. He probably slipped into the porter camp at night and is laying low."

"I hope so."

"And Sun-jo and Yash?" he asked.

"As far as I know they're in Nepal."

"What?"

I told him about Zopa's plan.

He broke into a broad grin. "That son of a . . . Captain Shek is going to flip when he finds out. Topping the mountain." He shook his head, then turned a little more serious.

"How far did you make it?"

"Above Camp Six."

"Well, you made it a lot farther than most people. I'll take you next year or the year after. We'll go up on the Nepal side. After Shek finds out about Sun-jo I'll never get a permit to climb on this side again. When did Sun-jo summit?"

"One thirty-two P.M. May thirtieth. A day before his fifteenth birthday."

He put his hand on my shoulder. "I wish it could have been you."

"No worries," I said.

"We go!" one of the soldiers said.

"In a minute!" Josh said, then turned back to me. "Shek is going to detain you when you get to Base Camp and ask you some questions. Thaddeus will be there with you. In real life Thaddeus is a lawyer and is fluent in Chinese and Chinese law. You'll be okay."

I *was* going to be okay, but not for the reason he thought.

And I was not going to join him on another Everest climb. I'd had enough of 8,000-meter peaks littered with corpses.

"I'm going home," I said.

"What do you mean?"

"Back to New York."

"We'll talk about that when I get back down."

"I won't be there when you get down," I said.

"What's the hurry?"

"You wouldn't understand."

"Try me."

"Okay. I want to be home for the twins' birthday."

By the look on his face I was right. He didn't understand.

"I haven't missed one yet," I said.

Josh stared at me for a moment. "Well, I guess Thaddeus can get you a ride to Kathmandu."

"We go now!" the Chinese soldier shouted.

"We're just about finished," Josh said irritably.

"I guess I'd better go."

"Yeah . . . well . . . Sorry it didn't work out." Josh put out his hand.

"Actually, it did work out," I said, shaking his hand. "I'll see you around."

I started following the soldiers and Yogi, then turned back and shouted, "Write when you get a chance."

Josh looked at me and grinned. "I might just do that."

WE GOT TO BASE CAMP about five o'clock. Captain Shek, several soldiers, and Thaddeus Bowen were waiting for me. They weren't interested in Yogi and let him go into camp.

When we got to Shek's headquarters, the first thing he

did was to dump everything in my pack onto a large table. Then (just like my New York detective a century ago) he examined the contents item by item.

He found nothing of interest except for the digital camera Josh had gotten for me, JR's video camera, and my Moleskine. He flipped through the Moleskine, found mostly blank pages, and put it back down. The cameras he pushed to the side of the table.

"Sit," he said.

There was a single straight-back chair.

I sat.

He asked me the same questions he had asked me up at Camp Four, but this time he had a tape recorder going and a soldier taking notes. I answered the questions in the exact same way. When he finished he told me I could repack my things. I began stuffing things back in, but when I got to the cameras the captain stopped me.

"Not those," he said.

"You have no right to take anything," Thaddeus said.

"Cameras will be returned after we look."

"Well, there better not be any damage to them when they are returned," Thaddeus said.

Some lawyer, I thought. *Glad he wasn't defending me when I was in front of that NYC judge. I'd be in jail right now.*

When we got outside the building he whispered, "Was there anything incriminating in those cameras?"

"It's a little bit late to be asking now," I said. "But the answer is no. I took the memory card out and put a blank one in."

"Where is the memory card?"

"Someplace safe." (It was actually stuffed in my sock.)

I was tired. I started toward my tent, and it wasn't until I got there that I remembered I didn't have a tent there anymore. I crawled into Josh's and I was a little surprised at how tidy everything was. All the clothes were neatly folded, gear stored in boxes. He had a little folding desk with pens, paper, and a laptop computer. Next to the computer were two stacks of mail. The first stack was addressed to him. The second stack was addressed to me. (My stack was a lot smaller than his.) I could have gotten mad again at the whole mail thing, but I didn't have the energy or the interest anymore. Like I said, "You don't get to pick your name or your parents." Joshua Wood is what he is. I couldn't change him or the fact he was my father. All I could do is try not to become him.

I opened the big envelope, addressed to PEAK "PEA-PEA" MARCELLO. Inside was a drawing and a smaller envelope. Written on the outside of the envelope was: AIRPLAN FAR (six-year-old spelling). Inside was sixty-seven dollars and eighty-six cents. Not quite enough to get to New York, but I still had Rolf's three hundred bucks, and the credit card. I pulled out the drawing. It was an invitation to a birthday party. I would have to hurry if I was going to make it in time.

I started toward HQ to find Thaddeus, but on the way I heard a truck start. I ran over to see if I could hitch a ride and found Yogi in the back.

The drivers charged me a hundred bucks but I didn't care. I would have paid twice as much. I was on my way home and the truck was nicer than the one we'd taken to the mountain. The covered bed was empty, with plenty of room to lie down and sleep.

The two drivers took turns at the wheel, and were both in a hurry. They only stopped for fuel. Which was fine with me.

WHEN WE CAME TO THE ROAD above the Friendship Bridge where the prisoners had been chipping the boulder, the truck slowed, then came to a stop.

Yogi and I hopped out of the back to find out what was going on.

The boulder and prisoners were gone. In their place was a Buddhist monk with a shaved head and an orange robe. He was talking to the driver with his back to us.

As we walked up, he turned around and smiled. It was Zopa! He looked fully recovered—as healthy as he had the first day I met him in the Indrayani temple.

"How did you get here?"

He held up his thumb. "I hitchhiked."

Somehow I doubted that. Why would someone drop him off on this lonely stretch of road? The only thing nearby was the border crossing at the Friendship Bridge. Unless he asked to be let out here. *I will see you on the road,* his note had said. I figured he had messed up the phrase and meant *down* the road. I guess I was wrong. The three of us got into the back of the truck.

I thought we were in for a big hassle at the bridge, but when we got there, the guards looked in our truck, glanced at our papers, then waved us through without a word.

We made one more stop before we got to the airport in Kathmandu. I complained that I needed to get to the airport, but Zopa made a good point: "They will not allow you on an airplane looking and smelling like you do."

The monks at the monastery washed my clothes as I took a long bath.

ZOPA RODE TO THE AIRPORT with me.

Before going into the terminal I pulled out the note Zopa had left for us at Camp Four.

"How did you know you'd see me on that road?"

Zopa shrugged. The answer didn't surprise me.

I unzipped a side pocket on my pack and pulled out the memory card. "You might need this to prove Sun-jo got to the summit."

Zopa took the card and stashed it in the folds of his orange robe. "Will we see you again on Sagarmatha?"

I wanted to shrug my reply, but I couldn't because I knew the answer. "No," I said. "But I might return to Kathmandu to visit."

"You are welcome anytime." Zopa bowed and gave me a blessing.

When he looked up he said, "Thank you for what you did for my grandson."

I returned the bow. "Thank you for what your son did for my father."

DENOUEMENT

IT TOOK TWENTY-FOUR HOURS to get to New York, but because I crossed the international date line going west, I got there only a few hours after I left Kathmandu.

I grabbed a cab and nervously fidgeted as the driver fought the heavy traffic into the city, hoping that I wouldn't be too late. When he pulled up in front of our building I gave him a fistful of cash without even counting it. I took the elevator to the loft.

I heard the party before I saw it. Rolf knew how to throw a party. (Mom and I were a little weak in that area.) There would be no less than seventy-five people in the loft: parents and their kids, teachers from GSS, neighbors, people from Mom's bookstore, lawyers from Rolf's office. . . . Last year for entertainment, Rolf had hired a group of performing dogs. The year before he had brought a reptile woman (Helen the Herpetologist—the twins' favorite) with bags of snakes, turtles, and lizards.

It turned out that I was the entertainment this year—at least that's what it looked like when I walked through the front door.

"I told you he would be here!"

"I did, too!"

The two Peas dropped their presents and threw their little arms around my thighs. Mom was next, then Rolf. I told myself that I wasn't going to cry, but that idea went right out the window as soon as I saw them. As we hugged, everyone sang "Happy Birthday."

When everything had settled down a little, Mom pulled me into the kitchen and asked me how I was. I told her I was tired and a little sore.

"You've lost weight."

"I guess."

She looked at me for a moment, then gave me another hug. "I'm glad you're back."

"Me too."

"So, you didn't make it to the summit."

"How'd you know that?"

"Josh called this morning. Said to tell you happy birthday."

That was a first. "Where was he?"

"He didn't say . . . somewhere up the mountain. The connection wasn't very good. It reminded me of the old days."

"I bet," I said. "I know I should have called, but I wanted it to be a surprise."

"It was still a surprise," Mom said. "I didn't think you'd get here in time for the birthday—although the two Peas insisted I was wrong."

"Is everything okay here . . . I mean is it all right that I came back?"

"Your skyscraper stunt is old news, and Rolf and I are trying to keep it that way."

"What do you mean 'trying'?"

"Holly Angelo."

"Uh-oh."

"She's been hanging around a lot."

"I'm sorry."

"No, it's okay. I kind of like her, and the twins are wild about her. Rolf? Well, he *tolerates* her. We've talked her into not writing about your Everest trip. It would just bring up the whole skyscraper thing again and we don't want to do that, especially now that you're back in town. It's best if we—"

Rolf opened the kitchen door with an apologetic, worried look on his face.

"Peeeeak!"

Holly pushed him aside as she assaulted the kitchen wearing a bright pink pantsuit, lime green scarf, and a red purse the size of a suitcase. I let her throw her spidery arms around me and actually hugged her back. It was good to see her.

When she finally set me free she glanced furtively around the kitchen as if she were looking for spies. "I heard you didn't make it to the summit," she whispered. "I'm sorry."

"How did *you* find out?"

"I've talked to Josh several times in the past couple days."

He was being pretty chatty, it seemed.

Holly put her red purse on the counter, looked around again, then pulled out a newspaper. "This is about to hit the streets."

YOUNGEST PERSON SUMMITS EVEREST BY HOLLY ANGELO. It was a full-page spread with several photos taken from video I had shot. The biggest photo was of Sun-jo, Yogi, and Yash sitting next to the summit pole.

"I think there's a book in this," Holly said. "I talked to Sun-jo today. He said to say hello and to wish you a happy birthday. He also told me he's enjoying the birthday present you gave him, and so are his sisters."

I smiled.

"What did you get him?" Holly asked.

"Nothing much," I said. "I'd better go out and mingle."

Rolf gave me a doubtful look.

I said hello to a few people, got a tour of the twins' presents, then noticed Vincent sitting in the corner by himself, gathering grist. I was surprised to see him. We always invited him to the parties, but he rarely showed up.

"Thanks for coming," I said.

"I was just about ready to leave when you walked through the door," Vincent said. "You have had an interesting few weeks."

"You read the Moleskine," I said.

"Yes, and it was well written. Unfortunately, there is only a beginning and a partial middle to the story. Even though you managed to fill the Moleskine I'm afraid the assignment is incomplete. The story lacks a climax, an end, and a denouement. So, I cannot—"

"There's a second Moleskine," I said. "I'm not sure about the climax, but the story does have an end . . . kind of. And I'm right in the middle of the denouement, literally." I pointed at the partygoers.

Vincent smiled. "Of course. I see your point."

"How about if I finish it up tomorrow morning?"

"That will be fine. I will be at GSS until noon. School is out for the summer and the deadline for your assignment has passed, but under the circumstances I think we can make an exception." He stood up. "And again, it's a well-crafted story. You left me hanging. I'm desperate to find out what happened."

I'M SITTING IN MY BEDROOM finishing the Moleskine.

The twins are awake. I hear them giggling and arguing as they eat their midmorning snack. I promised to take them to GSS with me when I drop off the Moleskine.

Here they come, their little feet pattering up the steps. The door opens.

"What are you doing?"

"You said you'd take us to school."

"I'm working on my assignment."

"What's this?" Patrice points at the newspaper article about Sun-jo pinned on my bulletin board.

"Is that you?" Paula asks, pointing at Sun-jo.

"No."

"What are those flags?"

"Prayer flags."

"What's a prayer flag?"

"There's a prayer written on the flag. When it blows in the wind the prayer goes up to God. If you put the flag really high on a mountain the prayer gets to God faster."

"Looks like that yellow one has a blue mountain on it like the ones you used to draw."

"It could be. Now, sit down on my bed and be quiet so I can finish this."

"We missed you, Peak."

"We love you, Peak."

"I love you, too. I'm almost finished."

I look at the twins, smiling, and write my last sentence . . .

The only thing you'll find on the summit of Mount Everest is a divine view. The things that really matter lie far below.

ACKNOWLEDGMENTS:

I want to thank Kate Harrison for her wonderful editing and encouragement, and for giving me the Os to finish the climb. I also want to thank Anne Davies, who has gone off to climb her own peak.